Evangelical Catechism

American Edition

Evangelical Catechism

Christian Faith in the World Today

American Edition

AUGSBURG Publishing House • Minneapolis

EVANGELICAL CATECHISM
American Edition

Library of Congress Catalog Card No. 82-70953
International Standard Book No. 0-8066-1928-7

Translation of *Evangelischer Gemeindekatechismus,*
copyright © 1979 United Evangelical Lutheran
Church of Germany, Hannover; published by Güter-
sloher Verlagshaus Gerd Mohn; edited by Horst Reller,
Hermann Müller, Martin Voigt.

American edition translated by Lawrence W. Denef
and adapted in consultation with Harold Ditmanson,
Irene Getz, Paul Jersild, Charles Lutz, Paul Martin-
son, Philip Quanbeck, Wayne Stumme, Mons Teig.

Manufactured in the United States of America

Contents

Acknowledgments

Scripture quotations unless otherwise noted are from the Revised Standard Version of the Bible, copyright 1946, 1952, and 1971 by the Division of Christian Education of the National Council of Churches.

Quotations from the Psalms are from *Standard Book of Common Prayer*, copyright 1977 by Charles Mortimer Guilbert as custodian. Used by permission.

English translation of the Lord's Prayer and the Apostles' and Nicene Creeds prepared by International Consultation on English Texts.

Quotations from the Lutheran Confessions are from the *Book of Concord*, translated and edited by Theodore G. Tappert, © 1959 by Fortress Press (formerly Muhlenberg Press).

The following material is from *Lutheran Book of Worship*, copyright © 1978: p. 27, Hymn 485, stanza 1; p. 50, Hymn 453, stanza 2; pp. 154-155, Hymn 228, stanza 3; pp. 199-200, Hymn 166, stanza 3; pp. 251-252, Prayer 200; pp. 301-302, Hymn 288, stanzas 1-2; p. 304, Prayer 230; pp. 370-371, Prayer 3.

The prayer by Dietrich Bonhoeffer on p. 13 is reprinted with permission of Macmillan Publishing Co., Inc. and SCM Press Ltd. from· *Letters and Papers from Prison* by Dietrich Bonhoeffer. Copyright © 1953, 1967, 1971 by SCM Press Ltd.

The hymn text on p. 231 is from "Come Holy Ghost, God and Lord," copyright 1941 by Concordia Publishing House. Used by permission. The hymn text on p. 386 is from "O Sacred Head Now Wounded," stanza 4 copyright 1941 Concordia Publishing House. Used by permission.

Photos: Jerry Davis, 16; Wallowitch, 19, 25, 43, 49, 141, 195, 294, 382; John Taylor, 22; Eric L. Wheater, 29, 46, 124, 261, 277, 343; Florence Sharp, 33, 245, 273; Les Myers, 36, 210; Tony Allegretti, 52; Rohn Engh, 59; Al Barry, 66; Robert Maust, 80, 106, 255; Bruce Jennings, 85; Jim Solheim, 102; Joanne Meldrum, 121, 192; Strix Pix, 126; Jack Hamilton, 137; Almasy, 150; RNS, 153, 179, 227; British Museum, 163; Roger W. Neal, 166, 286, 291, 311; Raynald Leblanc, 205, 360; Mark Gonnerman, 222; Dale G. Folstad, 238, 308; Dan R. Forbes, 258; Peter G. Aitken, 298, 376; Lisa A. Faneuf, 322; Diane M. Bellavia, 325; Church World Service, 331; Frederick D. Bodin, 348; Rick Smolan, 363; Paul M. Schrock, 366; Anne L. Nordmark, 379; H. Armstrong Roberts, 395.

Introduction

This is a book about the gospel. The gospel of Jesus Christ—the *evangel* or good news—is the treasure of the church, the content of its preaching and teaching, the heartbeat of its mission and service. An *evangelical* book is one that presents the good news of Jesus Christ as the very center of Christian faith and life and the standard by which all else is understood, explained, and judged.

This is a book for our time. It is a *catechism*, a summary of Christian teachings that communicates the content of faith in a contemporary and understandable way. Many catechisms have been written down through the centuries, including two by Martin Luther that remain influential to this day. The purpose of this *Evangelical Catechism* is to relate the gospel of Jesus Christ to the needs and challenges of modern life.

The history of this book begins in 1969, when the United Evangelical Lutheran Church of Germany, under the leadership of Bishop Hanns Lilje, established a commission to develop a new catechism. The churches sensed an urgent need for a book to present Christian faith in the light of modern scientific insights and contemporary problems. Members of the commission consulted not only pastors and theologians, but also more than 200 representatives from all major walks of life and such professions as medicine, law, business, and psychology. The text of the emerging book was field-tested by 35 different groups of people.

Out of this process developed a large and excellent book based on experience and the living discussion of pastoral problems and intellectual difficulties. That new catechism *(Evangelischer Erwachsenenkatechismus)* was published in 1975. The German Lutheran churches have also published several additional books based on the catechism project. One of these is *A Book of Christian Faith* by Johann Christoph Hampe (Augsburg, 1980). That book is primarily addressed to individual readers, especially those who have serious doubts about the Christian faith.

Evangelical Catechism is the second volume based on the new German catechism to appear in English. This book is intended for both individual and group study. It is for those who already have a foundation of Christian faith and desire more in-depth study, reflection, sharing, and discussion. This catechism presents a consensus of basic Christian teachings and invites readers to explore the relationship between faith and life. It offers an approach to the many different topics of Christian faith; it is a tool for helping Christians think through the meaning of the gospel; and it provides an opportunity for group study.

Evangelical Catechism begins with human experience. Part One is titled, "Who Am I?" and provides a brief sketch of the many dimensions of human life. With this context in mind, Parts Two through Five present the topics of God, sin, Jesus, and the Holy Spirit. Part Six discusses how Christians live in the world, and Part Seven points to the future completion of God's kingdom. The whole book attempts to move beyond mere information to reflection, discussion, and personal appropriation. Luther's catechetical question, "What does this mean for us?" is a constant theme.

Summary statements at the end of each chapter review the content. In addition, six quotations are provided for reflection. The first is always a passage from Scripture, the last is always a prayer, and a hymn is always included. Other quotations from Christian writers throughout history sharpen the questions raised in the chapter. Dates of birth and death are given for all except living authors.

This American Edition has been translated, field-tested, revised, and adapted by a team of Americans to meet the needs of the English-speaking world. Leadership in the development of the American Edition has been provided by the Division for Life and Mission in the Congregation and the Division for Theological Education and Ministry of the American Lutheran Church.

A variety of resources and materials have been helpful in this process. For example, the majority of the quotations in the "For Reflection" sections are drawn from books published in English by authors familiar to English-speaking Christians. In addition, some policy statements and guidelines of the American Lutheran Church have been adapted to supplement certain sections, especially Chapters 18-21.

This volume is not intended to replace Luther's Small and Large Catechisms. Those classic explanations of Christian faith are part of the church's confessional heritage and will always have an important place. Building on the foundation of the church's evangelical and confessional tradition, this catechism provides a contemporary understanding of Christian teachings. Its purpose is to help readers participate in a living discussion of Christian faith and life for our time.

The text of the book includes many Bible quotations and Scripture references. These are usually from the Revised Standard Version, although the Psalms are from the *Standard Book of Common Prayer* (the same version used in *Lutheran Book of Worship*). The references provide an overview of biblical teaching, but they are not exhaustive. Those who read, study, and discuss this book will find it an important contribution to a lifetime of faith and learning.

Part One

Who Am I?

Who am I? They often tell me
I would step from my cell's confinement
calmly, cheerfully, firmly,
like a squire from his country-house. . . .

Am I then really all that which other men tell of?
Or am I only what I know of myself,
restless and longing and sick, like a bird in a cage. . .?

Who am I? This or the other?
Am I one person today, and tomorrow another?
Am I both at once? . . .

Who am I? They mock me, these lonely questions of mine.
Whoever I am, thou knowest, O God, I am thine.

Dietrich Bonhoeffer (1906-1945)
Letters and Papers from Prison
(Macmillan, 1971), pp. 347-348

1

Creature and Partner

Human beings often ask themselves the question, Who am I? Myths, religions, and cults show us how people have reflected on their lives, discovered their possibilities and limitations, and portrayed the frightening powers of the unknown in pictures and symbols. The question of who we are is an ever-present part of life. It cuts through the commonplace and challenges our very existence as persons.

Do we come to understand ourselves through relationships with others, or through the challenges of life? Or do we truly find ourselves only when we encounter God? How do we discover who we really are?

1. How do others view me?

When other people describe who we are, they can use the insights of biology, law, psychology, sociology, religion, or other disciplines. The diversity of these approaches illustrates the diversity that exists within us.

Viewed *biologically,* you are the son or daughter of

your natural parents. You may have inherited the posture of your father or the eyes of your mother. You may have facial features similar to your grandmother and the hair color of an aunt. You can probably trace your family tree through several generations before it disappears into the unknown. Genetic research indicates you are a single combination of factors out of some 500,000,000 different possibilities. All the cells in your body (except those in your brain) are renewed every seven years. You change, yet you stay the same person.

The cells in your body are developed out of the same substances as those of all living creatures on earth. Your body is subject to the same developmental laws that govern every organism: birth, growth, maturity, aging, death. You are one of many living creatures, all living under the same laws of nature. But how many variations there are within this uniformity! You belong to a single species among the multitudes of living creatures, and so are distinguishable from all other species. Yet even within your own species—which biologists call *Homo sapiens*—you bear distinctive characteristics, such as skin color and life expectancy.

Nevertheless, the question, Who am I? has not yet been answered. In fact only now do the many characteristics that distinguish you from others first come into view. For example, you may be strong, physically healthy, and disease resistant; or you may be weak, ill, or physically handicapped. Even characteristics like these are only the beginning of your identity.

Viewed *legally,* you are recognized as an individual when your birth is registered at a government office. This assures that you have legal standing according to the laws of your country. When you are involved in activities of a legal nature you must prove your identity on the basis of your birth certificate or passport.

From the moment of your birth you can own property. Even before your birth, the law says you hold the right of inheritance. At a certain age, you are considered legally competent to engage in business transactions. You can vote, sign contracts, and be punished for crimes.

Viewed *psychologically* or *sociologically,* you are shaped by your surroundings, your history, and your involvement in the human world. The impressions of your early childhood are especially important. There were persons who gave you life and from whom you received your self-consciousness and sense of direction. There were the sounds of the language you heard early and learned to speak. There were your first experiences of being welcomed into the world or being rejected, being surrounded by love and joy or being shoved aside by others. In what kind of a world (spiritual, intellectual, social) did you grow up? Was it a world of bright colors or one filled with gloomy tones, a world of poverty or affluence? Your relationships with your father, mother, sisters or brothers,

and the environment that first shaped you influence your educational development, choice of occupation, and selection of a mate.

What you have learned during your years in school is a result of thousands of years of human cultural development in areas such as language, literature, mathematics, and monetary systems. You assume roles in a variety of life situations, each role having its own expected behavior. These enable you to become involved with different groups of persons and initiate relationships. As an adult you play your role as a worker, executive, clerk, family member, sports participant, church member, or member of a political party. You are part of a particular country, a particular people, and a particular era.

Your individual destiny is found within a host of common destinies. You have not selected the time in which you live. Changes in the forms and structures underlying your time, your century, and finally, world history itself shape much of your future.

Viewed *religiously*, you are a creature who experiences life on more than one level. Your senses of sight, smell, hearing, taste, and touch connect you with other people and with the objects that surround you. You can enjoy yourself, become angry, laugh, or cry. You can also reflect deeply on yourself and on the world. Although you cannot be separated into different "parts" such as body, soul, and spirit, terms like these express the fact that you experience life in different ways. Each way opens a different door to your whole person.

You have religious views and commitments. You have grown up in a community with a particular religious or philosophical outlook. This has shaped your attitudes, your sense of values, and your conduct. Perhaps your parents considered themselves non-religious. Still, they had their own values, longings, and hopes that contributed to your formation.

2. How do I view myself?

Descriptions of our background, qualities, and surroundings do not provide a complete answer to the question, Who am I? Inherited traits and the influence of our environment have been bonded together into our own individuality. We respond to life through our attitudes and behavior patterns.

This response may be expressed in the form of constant dissatisfaction: we look begrudgingly at others who are wealthier, more beautiful, more carefree, who have a happier disposition, for whom everything seems to go well. We are disturbed that we are not the people we would like to be. We may blame ourselves for the way we are and become caught up in self-accusations. We may blame those around us, circumstances, fate, or God.

Such dissatisfaction is unrealistic. Every life has its crises and shadows, and all of us can discover something good about ourselves. Dissatisfaction is also

unproductive. If we reject ourselves because of our failures, we become blind to the possibilities that are also part of our lives. If we constantly look for the reasons behind our plight, we only run around in circles. Instead of taking advantage of life's opportunities, we see only our misfortune in every new turn of events.

The response that opens up possibilities for the future is trust. We accept what we have been given and acknowledge what we have done with it. Since we cannot start from scratch, we need to orient ourselves to our own personal history. To the degree that we assume responsibility for our own history, we also become capable of bearing responsibility for our future.

We human beings follow tortuous and puzzling paths on our way to self-discovery. It is not always possible to set our course at the beginning of our adult lives and easily reach our final destination. We do not always know where the future will take us when we step out in trust. This is not necessarily bad. A Portuguese proverb says, "Even on crooked lines, God writes straight." Side paths can bring new insights and directions—when we are open to learning from them.

3. How does God view me?

During the course of our life we assume many roles. To each we contribute some time and energy. No one role reveals our entire selves. But can we identify one fundamental role to help us understand and arrange all the others?

We come to know ourselves through relationships with others. We begin to discover our identity as we meet others who accept us the way we are, with all our imperfections, weaknesses, and doubts. When we respond to this kind of acceptance we begin the process of trust and open doors into the future. We begin to answer the question, Who am I? when we experience unconditional love and pass it on to others.

The love we receive and pass on points beyond itself to the love of God, who is the source of all acceptance and trust. We are not only dependent on other people, but also on God. And our relationship to God is based on God's relationship with us.

God has created each of us as a unique creature. None of us occurs a second time among the other four and one-half billion members of the human race. Each of us has been created to have a relationship with God as a partner in the created world.

Who am I? God tells us who we are. We are his creatures and partners whom he loves.

Summary

- The question of who we are is an ever-present part of life.
- We respond to life by the attitudes we display and through our behavior patterns.

- The response that opens up possibilities for the future is trust.
- We come to know ourselves through relationships with others.
- God has created each of us as a unique creature.
- God tells us who we are. We are his creatures and partners whom he loves.

For reflection

Lord, you have searched me out and known me;
you know my sitting down and my rising up;
you discern my thoughts from afar.
You trace my journeys and my resting-places
and are acquainted with all my ways.
Indeed, there is not a word on my lips,
but you, O Lord, know it altogether.
You press upon me behind and before
and lay your hand upon me.
Such knowledge is too wonderful for me;
it is so high that I cannot attain to it.
Where can I go then from your Spirit?
Where can I flee from your presence?
If I climb up to heaven, you are there;
if I make the grave my bed, you are there also.

How deep I find your thoughts, O God!
How great is the sum of them!
If I were to count them,
they would be more in number than the sand;

to count them all, my life span would need
to be like yours.

Search me out, O God, and know my heart;
try me and know my restless thoughts.
Look well whether there be any wickedness in me,
and lead me in the way that is everlasting.

  Ps. 139:1-7, 16-17, 22-23

Lord, as a pilgrim
through life I go;
Each day your loving
presence I know.
Travel beside me,
Strengthen and guide me,
Shepherd divine!

  Wilhelmi Malmivaara (1854-1922)
  Lutheran Book of Worship 485

God's cry of creation does not call to the soul, but
to the wholeness of things. . . . Man stands created, a
whole body, ensouled by his relation to the created,
enspirited by his relation to the Creator. It is to the
whole man, in this unity of body, soul, and spirit, that
the Lord of Revelation comes and upon whom he lays
his message. So it is not only with his thought and his

feelings, but with the sole of his foot and the tip of his finger as well, that he may receive the sign-language of the reality taking place.

Martin Buber (1878-1965)
Israel and the World
(Schocken, 1948), p. 27

We have all forgotten what we really are. All that we call common sense and rationality and practicality and positivism only means that for certain dead levels of our life we forget that we have forgotten. All that we call spirit and art and ecstasy only means that for one awful instant we remember that we forget.

G. K. Chesterton (1874-1936)
Orthodoxy
(Dodd, Mead and Co., 1908), p. 97

Each and every one of us is irreplaceable, like a unique masterpiece in a collection, for God is an artist who never repeats or copies Himself. Neither a leaf nor a person's fingerprints are ever the same, and this is true also of the soul: it is always unique. And a soul that is lost is never duplicated in all eternity, and God feels this loss eternally. God loves each and every one of us more than we love ourselves.

Ernesto Cardenal

To Live Is To Love
(Herder & Herder, 1972), p. 43

Lord, I've been wondering:
Why do I say *I?*
Why must I ask why?
Why is joy so close to pain?
Why do I feel transparent
in the presence of a child?
Why am I so often lonely in a crowd?
Why are people so sober before a clock?
And a ten dollar bill?
Why am I so loud when I'm wrong?
Or so fierce when I'm afraid?
Why is the human face most beautiful
when it is looking up?
Why, in moments of crisis,
do people either curse or pray?
Why does prosperity drive us apart?
And adversity bring us together?
Why is it painful to celebrate alone?
Why does my ability to ask questions
exceed my capacity to receive answers?
Why am I a mystery even to myself?
Lord, give me the right questions,
and bless my growing.

Gerhard E. Frost
Bless My Growing
(Augsburg, 1974), p. 28

2

Freedom and Limitation

Liberation is a word often heard today. The human longing for liberation is very old and very deep. We want lives free of hunger, poverty, domination, violence, and ignorance. We have the freedom to make decisions and to act. Despite this, we experience painful limitations. What holds us in bondage? How can we find real freedom?

1. What do the social sciences say?

We do not enter the world like blank sheets of paper on which we can write whatever we want. From our parents we have inherited hereditary factors that affect everything from our bodily structures to our capacities for thinking.

We are also powerfully influenced by instincts such as sexuality and aggression. Much of our behavior can be understood as the result of the interaction between our instincts and our environment. Many times we do not consciously control our actions, but simply react to external circumstances.

Human beings are also linguistically conditioned;

31

along with language we receive the basic patterns and values of our culture. Through language we are able to discover ourselves, experience community with others, and understand the world. Where the capacity of language is stunted, persons themselves can be stunted.

We are dependent on:

- our body as conditioned by nature
- nature as a whole
- our surroundings in the broadest sense
- the persons with whom we associate
- our own past

The fact that we are limited and dependent does not mean we cannot change. We are capable of shaping our lives as persons as well as being shaped by outside influences.

Biologically, it can be demonstrated that human beings are much less fixed than animals. While animals are guided almost exclusively by their instincts, we have the ability to control our instincts. In addition, we can use our minds to understand the laws of nature. This ability makes it possible to develop tools and shape our surroundings.

Families are examples of the human ability to structure the surrounding social world. We develop and change in our relationships with others. We are able not only to adjust to changing circumstances, but also to alter them. Life holds many possibilities to be discovered and developed.

2. What does the Bible say?

We were created to be free

So God created man in his own image, in the image of God he created him; male and female he created them. And God blessed them, and God said to them, "Be fruitful and multiply, and fill the earth and subdue it; and have dominion over the fish in the sea and over the birds in the air and over every living thing that moves upon the earth" (Gen. 1:27-28).

Note how the theme of freedom is taken up in this biblical account of creation. The fact that God has created human beings in his own image indicates two things:

● Human beings are called to be "stewards of God," to represent the rule of God in the world.

● God created human beings to be in relationship with him. We find our fulfillment only within the bonds of a relationship with God.

God's intention for us is expressed by the psalmist as he looks in wonder at the world God has created:

When I consider your heavens, the work of your fingers,
the moon and the stars you have set in their courses,
what is man that you should be mindful of him,
the son of man that you should seek him out?
You have made him but little lower than the angels;
you adorn him with glory and honor . . . (Ps. 8:4-6).

We are not free

Human beings were created not for slavery but for freedom. Yet we consistently abandon the relationship God intends for us. We think we will find freedom through independence. Instead of giving us freedom, our rebellion leads us into slavery to ourselves. This slavery to our own wills and desires is what Luther called the "bondage of the will." St. Paul described the feeling of slavery when he said, "I can will what is right, but I cannot do it. For I do not do the good I want, but the evil I do not want is what I do" (Rom. 7:18-19).

We find the freedom God intends for us only when God brings us back into a relationship with himself:

It is also taught among us that man possesses some measure of freedom of the will which enables him to live an outwardly honorable life and to make choices among the things that reason comprehends. But without the grace, help, and activity of the Holy Spirit man is not capable of making himself acceptable to God, of fearing God and believing in God with his whole heart, or of expelling inborn evil lusts from his heart. This is accomplished by the Holy Spirit, who is given through the Word of God (Augsburg Confession, *Book of Concord*, p. 39).

3. What are the limits to freedom?

Theological statements about the bondage of the will do not mean there is no human freedom. We are

free to make decisions and act in everyday affairs. Yet we are in slavery because apart from God, we make decisions to suit our ends, not his. Our actions are not determined, but apart from a relationship with God we are "turned inward upon ourselves" in all we do.

Christ made it possible for us to be freed from slavery to ourselves. With the kind of freedom he gives us we can refuse to become dependent on things, power, jobs, or systems. We can avoid elevating ourselves or others to positions of ultimate authority. We can place our lives and our futures in the hands of God alone.

Our freedom is not just a freedom *from*, but also a freedom *for*: "A Christian is a perfectly free lord of all, subject to none. A Christian is a perfectly dutiful servant of all, subject to all" (Martin Luther, *Luther's Works*, vol. 31, Fortress, p. 344).

The boundary of our freedom is established by the freedom of others. It is love that limits our freedom. It is our relationship with God and our dependence on him that sets us free to serve others.

Summary

- We are dependent on our body, nature, our surroundings, others, and our own past.
- We are capable of shaping our lives and the world.

● Human beings are called to be "stewards of God," to represent the rule of God in the world.

● God created human beings to be in relationship with him.

● We find the freedom God intends for us only when God brings us back into a relationship with himself.

● The boundary of our freedom is established by the freedom of others. It is love that limits our freedom.

For reflection

For you were called to freedom, brethren; only do not use your freedom as an opportunity for the flesh, but through love be servants of one another. For the whole law is fulfilled in one word, "You shall love your neighbor as yourself."

Gal. 5:13-14

The King of love my shepherd is,
Whose goodness faileth never;
I nothing lack if I am his
And he is mine forever.

Henry W. Baker (1821-1877)
Lutheran Book of Worship 456

Man is a historical being. He is not born in the world of things, persons, and time as a finished product. His being is not prior to history. He becomes what he is through the history of his relations with his environment. He is not, therefore, simply a being *in* the world; he comes into being *with* the world.

Rubem Alves
A Theology of Human Hope
(Corpus, 1966), p. 3

Freedom is a quality in people that they acquire through a growth process that continues throughout their entire lives. Therefore to be mature implies that one is also free and implies also a constant self-improvement. The problem is how to grow, how to continue acquiring that maturity in life. . . . Love is the crux of our life and what makes our freedom develop.

Segundo Galilea
Following Jesus
(Orbis, 1981), p. 86

Changing the human heart and changing human society are not separate tasks, but are as interconnected as the two beams of the cross.

Henri Nouwen
The Wounded Healer
(Doubleday, 1972), p. 20

I thank thee, God, and like a child
Rejoice as for a Christmas gift,
That I am living—just alive—
Just for this human face I wear,
That I can see the sun, the sea,
The hills and grass and leafy trees,
And walk beneath the host of stars
And watch the lovely moon above.

Matthias Claudius (1740-1815)
How the World Began, by Helmut Thielicke, p. 28
© 1961 by Fortress Press
Reprinted by permission of Fortress Press

3

Happiness and Suffering

"Happiness" is something we desire and pursue, but what exactly is it? Happiness can be a slice of bread, the love between husband and wife, the first cry of a baby, moving into a new home, buying a long-desired item; it can even be the rejection of what is usually called happiness in order to avoid disappointment.

We learn from experience that whoever lives must also suffer. Suffering is part of life, along with working and resting, eating and drinking. Just as we are not asked if we want to be born or if we want to die, neither are we asked if we want to suffer. How are suffering and happiness related?

1. Is happiness a childhood dream?

If we see happiness as a special favor granted to some and not others, we would only be prudent if we prepared ourselves for disappointment. Actually it is part of a lingering childhood in us that longs for special favors, to have more than others, to receive more loving attention, to be better off than others—even at their expense.

When we understand the selfishness of striving for this kind of happiness, we have begun to mature. We realize that such happiness is not often found. We learn to distinguish between pleasure, desire, profit, preference, and true happiness. We become suspicious of the "big prize" pursued by those with happiness mania. We also become suspicious of superficial worldly pleasures.

The Greek philosopher Heraclitus warned long ago, "If happiness consists solely in bodily gratification, one would have to call the oxen happy when they find peas to eat." As we mature there is something in us that resists such simplistic notions of happiness.

Other persons—neighbors—are essential to human happiness. The isolation and loneliness of people today is a tragedy. Human happiness requires love between persons. If a husband and wife are happy, it is not because they won a sweepstakes. Their happiness comes from a relationship of mutual sharing. All of us yearn for the feeling of being supported and secure. Every time we experience it we know what true happiness is.

The source of real happiness is illustrated by the biblical story of Solomon's dream (1 Kings 3:5-15). God appeared to Solomon at Gibeon in a dream and said, "Ask what I shall give you." Solomon hesitated, then he said: "Give thy servant . . . an understanding mind to govern thy people, that I may discern be-

tween good and evil." The Lord was pleased with this prayer because Solomon did not request long life or riches for himself or the death of his enemies. He did not ask for the things most people consider essential for happiness. Instead he asked for discernment and wisdom, two more permanent and satisfying gifts.

2. Is suffering a curse?

We are often convinced that life is going well when we are successful and our wishes are fulfilled. We keep on hoping that our lives will become orderly and settled after our present difficulties are overcome, pains removed, and dangers eliminated.

We do not know why so many mysterious and often frightening things happen. And we do not understand how the ambiguities and terrors of this world can be reconciled with God's love.

We trust that God will one day explain all that is now incomprehensible and senseless. But we are not always able to maintain this kind of trust. Sometimes we simply feel abandoned and alone.

The afflictions of human beings are many and various. Suffering implies an encounter with chaos and senselessness. It calls into question what we have previously taken for granted. It diminishes our powers and abilities, damages our spirits and bodies. It takes away the people and things most dear to us. Suffering and love are connected. The more we love someone or something, the more we suffer when they are taken away. The greater our love, the more senseless is our suffering and the more alone we feel when we have lost what is dear to us.

Suffering is always something very personal. Each of us bears our pain alone. Suffering is an assignment that cannot be taken over by a substitute, even though much support can come from others.

Christians know they are included in the communion of those who suffer. The Gospels tell us Jesus was acquainted with suffering, all the way to the cross. He did not choose the path of suffering, but he accepted it: "Father, if thou art willing, remove this cup from me; nevertheless not my will, but thine, be done" (Luke 22:42). Jesus' suffering was not simply a surrender to unalterable fate, but rather a deliberate laying down of his life in obedience and trust.

Suffering is the sign by which we can recognize the bringer of salvation: "For the Son of man also came not to be served but to serve, and to give his life as a ransom for many" (Mark 10:45). Only by enduring suffering was Jesus able to restore wholeness to the world. New life, new ways of thinking, and new persons, according to the New Testament, are never brought into being by greatness or power, but only through tribulation. The world cannot be completely restored by concentrated attempts at mastering its problems, but only through suffering service and sacrificial love.

The suffering of Christians is a sign of their relationship with Christ: "We are afflicted in every way,

but not crushed; perplexed, but not driven to despair; persecuted, but not forsaken; struck down, but not destroyed; always carrying in the body the death of Jesus, so that the life of Jesus may also be manifested in our bodies" (2 Cor. 4:8-10). To be a Christian is to be united with Christ in his suffering, and yet to know that out of suffering God is bringing new life.

People react to suffering in different ways. Sometimes we react with anger and indignation. Other times we accept it in silence. Those who resist growing older, avoid new situations, reject new assignments, or deny times when their physical strength or personal means are no longer adequate, do not find peace, patience, or wisdom. They are unable to let go of the past and accept the future. They become rigid and inflexible. It is helpful to know that growth, maturation, and increased understanding rarely happen without the pain of leaving something behind.

We should be cautious about speaking too quickly and matter-of-factly about the blessings of suffering, or saying that God sends us suffering. But we can believe that God is able to use even destructive or demoralizing experiences as a means to help us grow in faith and understanding. "We know that in everything God works for good with those who love him, who are called according to his purpose" (Rom. 8:28). We are also much better equipped to help others when we ourselves have experienced suffering. It is hard to be sympathetic when we do not know what suffering is like.

Summary

- Other persons are essential to human happiness.
- Suffering calls into question what we have previously taken for granted.
- Suffering is always something very personal.
- Christians know they are included in the communion of those who suffer.
- The world is completely restored only through suffering service and sacrificial love.
- Growth, maturation, and increased understanding rarely happen without the pain of leaving something behind.

For reflection

For everything there is a season,
and a time for every matter under heaven:

a time to be born, and a time to die;
a time to plant, and a time to pluck up what is planted;
a time to kill, and a time to heal;
a time to break down, and a time to build up;
a time to weep, and a time to laugh;
a time to mourn, and a time to dance . . .
a time to seek, and a time to lose;
a time to keep, and a time to cast away. . . .

Eccles. 3:1-4, 6

What gain is there in futile weeping,
In helpless anger and distress?
If you are in his care and keeping,
In sorrow will he love you less?
For he who took for you a cross
Will bring you safe through ev'ry loss.

Georg Neumark (1621-1681)
Lutheran Book of Worship 453

God's great design is at present not to delight us
with pleasant experiences, but to exercise us as
His faithful people. Let me, therefore, trust God for
the pleasant things as realities laid up in reversion:
for I know they will come in all their fulness by and
by, with eternity. As little children give their sweet-
meats to their parents to keep for them, so my pleasant things are safer in God's keeping than in that of
my own treacherous heart. Forgetting the past, and
not taking thought for the morrow, I stand before
God today as His daily pensioner.

John Albert Bengel (1687-1752)
Gnomon of the New Testament, vol. v
(T. & T. Clark, 1863), p. xxx

One night a man became lost in the forest. His
lamp went out. Suddenly he came upon a wall of rock

and could go no further. He prayed: "Lord, take away this stone with an earthquake, so that I can move on." But there was no earthquake. Everything remained motionless. Instead, something quite different happened: the moon arose, and at once the wanderer saw the world in a new light. The stone was not cleared out of the way, but the wanderer was now able to find the way despite the stone. So it is also with the gift of the Holy Spirit. Our sore foot may not be healed. A particular stone of sorrow may not be cleared out of our way. But the Holy Spirit is a light upon our way, and brings us home despite all of these obstacles.

Story from Papua New Guinea

Is life so wretched? Isn't it rather your hands which are too small, your vision which is muddled? You are the one who must grow up.

We are not permitted to choose the frame of our destiny. But what we put into it is ours. He who wills adventure will experience it—according to the measure of his courage. He who wills sacrifice will be sacrificed—according to the measure of his purity of heart.

Dag Hammarskjöld (1905-1961)
Markings
(Alfred A. Knopf, 1964), p. 55

O Lord, Creator,
Ruler of the world, Father,
I thank, thank, thank you
that you have brought me through.
How strong the pain was—
but you were stronger.
How deep the fall was—
but you were even deeper.
How dark was the night—
but you were the noonday sun in it.
You are our father,
our mother,
our brother, and our friend.
Your grace has no end,
and your light no snuffer.
We praise you,
we honor you,
and we pray to your holy name.
We thank you
that you rule thus,
and that you are so merciful
with your tired followers.
Praised be you
through our Lord Jesus Christ.
Amen.

African prayer, Fritz Pawelzik, ed.
I Lie on My Mat and Pray
(© 1964 by Friendship Press), p. 40
Used by permission.

Part Two

Who Is God?

A god is that to which we look for all good and in which we find refuge in every time of need. To have a god is nothing less than to trust and believe him with our whole heart. As I have often said, the trust and faith of the heart alone make both God and an idol. If your faith and trust are right, then your God is the true God. On the other hand, if your trust is false and wrong, then you have not the true God. For these two belong together, faith and God. That to which your heart clings and entrusts itself is, I say, really your God.

Martin Luther (1483-1546)
Large Catechism, *Book of Concord*
(Fortress, 1959), p. 365

4

History and Revelation

We human beings are always trying to make sense out of our lives and our world. We are looking for something that ties all our experiences together. We would like to understand the supreme or ultimate reality that exists behind everything else in the universe. Is this reality a collection of mechanical forces, or is it a person? Does it help us or threaten us? Does it only issue commands, or does it also care for us? What is this reality? Is it God? Who is God?

1. What do we mean by God?

When we talk about God, we need to admit that people put their trust in many different gods. Luther said our god is whatever we trust the most. In this sense everyone could be called "religious," since all of us put our trust in something. Often we put complete trust only in ourselves. Sometimes we worship power, possessions, or pleasure. Another person can also become our god.

None of these things, however, can properly be called God. They are earthly things, part of the created world. When we try to put them in God's place they become idols. It is very important that we try to discover who God really is. Otherwise we may put our trust in something that is empty, fragile, deceptive, or transitory. We may live out our lives with a kind of naive optimism that our little gods will carry us through, only to find out we have been worshiping idols.

How is God to be distinguished from all other gods and idols? How can we find the true God among all the false gods? God is by definition the supreme or ultimate reality behind all things. If this reality is just a collection of mechanical forces, it may be an object for science and not for trust. On the other hand, if this reality is a being who can relate to us, then trust is possible, and to have any other god is idolatry.

2. Does God make himself known to us?

Christian faith believes God is greater than anything we can possibly imagine. He is the Creator of the universe, of all that exists. God's own thoughts are the foundation for the cosmos. Einstein compared God to a mathematician, someone who creates the very concepts on which all things are based.

At the same time, Christian faith insists that God is involved in the world. God has chosen to make him-

self known, even though his greatness is beyond all human knowing. He has spoken through human beings and the history of the people of Israel. His self-revelation is preserved in books written in Hebrew and Greek, languages whose images and metaphors seem strange to us.

Must our lives be bound to the history of an ancient people and their religious books? This may seem offensive in an age of science. Yet the Christian faith insists this is the way God has chosen to reveal himself.

What are we to make of the images, stories, and experiences recorded in the Bible? The Bible does not give us a comprehensive system of thought, a complete explanation for all reality. The stories and prayers, the characters and experiences of the Bible are like lenses we can use to recognize God and respond to him. According to the Bible, the center of all reality is God's call and our human response. If we want to know God today, there is no getting around the Bible. It is indispensable.

When we try to describe God, we use a form of technical language, the language of theology. But when we want to help another person come to know God, nothing can improve on the language of metaphors. The Bible's presentations of God do not capture him the way a photograph captures its subject. Instead, they communicate experiences people have had with God. They speak from one person's life to another's in a deep and powerful way. For this reason it is not wise to strip the Bible of all its images. Instead, we need to make the language of metaphors available once again to people who have been bombarded with commercial and technological language. Our language needs to be enriched by the Bible and its images.

3. How does the Bible describe encounters with God?

I love you, O Lord my strength,
O Lord my stronghold, my crag, and my haven.
My God, my rock in whom I put my trust,
my shield, the horn of my salvation,
and my refuge . . . (Ps. 18:1-2).

In the Bible people call on God using a variety of titles. Each title shows what the person expects to receive from God. The name *Yahweh* ("I am who I am" or "I will be whom I will be") distinguished the God of Israel from all the other gods of that time. This was the mysterious name given to Moses when he encountered God in the burning bush (Exodus 3). Later in Israel's history this name was held in such reverence that it was no longer spoken. It was replaced by the phrase "the Lord." Most English Bibles follow this tradition.

Calling on God sometimes appeared useless:

O my God, I cry in the daytime,
but you do not answer;
by night as well, but I find no rest (Ps. 22:2).

The opposite was also true. Sometimes people wanted to escape God's overwhelming call:

O Lord, thou hast deceived me,
and I was deceived;
thou art stronger than I,
and thou hast prevailed.
I have become a laughingstock all the day;
every one mocks me. . . .
If I say, "I will not mention him,
or speak any more in his name,"
there is in my heart as it were a burning fire
shut up in my bones,
and I am weary with holding it in,
and I cannot (Jer. 20:7, 9).

Sometimes the Bible talks about God in the third person, using images, allegories, allusions, or symbols:

Who is like the Lord our God,
who sits enthroned on high,
but stoops to behold
the heavens and the earth? (Ps. 113:5-6)

God is love, and he who abides in love abides in God, and God abides in him (1 John 4:16).

God is light and in him is no darkness at all (1 John 1:5).

Descriptions, images, and concepts about God are appropriate only when they point beyond themselves to an encounter with God. Taken literally, they can be false and misleading. This is made clear in the Old Testament prohibition of graven images:

> You shall not make for yourself a graven image, or any likeness of anything that is in heaven above, or that is in the earth beneath, or that is in the water under the earth; you shall not bow down to them or serve them; for I the Lord your God am a jealous God (Exod. 20:4-5).

Knowledge about God was transmitted by pointing to one's own experiences as well as to the experiences of others. People told stories of how God had helped them. Others listened and found hope that God could also help them. They called on God in prayer and praise, trusting him as the Lord of their lives. In this way they came to know God.

The Bible is filled with the stories of people who encountered God. They met him in circumstances that called their lives into question, gave them new direction, and strengthened them. The Bible bears witness that God is found by those who take the risk of trusting their lives to him.

4. How does the Bible describe God's actions?

God called a people

In the Old Testament, God's promises have to do with the people of Israel. It is usually the entire people who are addressed:

Hear, O Israel: The Lord our God is one Lord; and you shall love the Lord your God with all your heart, and with all your soul, and with all your might (Deut. 6:4-5).

The people of Israel experienced God not as an idea, but as someone with a will. They were chosen by this will of God, established by it, and confronted by it:

You only have I known
of all the families of the earth;
therefore I will punish you
for all your iniquities (Amos 3:2).

Israel was established as God's people by the deliverance from slavery in Egypt. The events surrounding this deliverance—the wilderness wanderings, the giving of the law, and the gift of the land—were the formative events in Israel's life. From the outside, God's choosing of Israel may seem to have been an arbitrary act, but for Israel it was an expression of undeserved love.

Not only did God choose Israel, but he made a covenant with his people, an agreement that expected an appropriate response to his love:

I am the Lord your God, who brought you out of the land of Egypt, out of the house of bondage. You shall have no other gods before me (Exod. 20:2-3).

With the faithful
you show yourself faithful, O God;
with the forthright you show yourself forthright.
With the pure you show yourself pure,
but with the crooked you are wily (Ps. 18:26-27).

The God Israel learned to know through its history
was not a God who remained untouched or unmoved
by human beings, a God exalted above history. God
is involved in history. That is why we can speak of
God's love and anger, passion and repentance.

How can I hand you over, O Israel! . . .
My heart recoils within me,
my compassion grows warm and tender.
I will not execute my fierce anger,
I will not again destroy Ephraim;
for I am God and not man,
the Holy One in your midst,
and I will not come to destroy (Hos. 11:8-9).

Israel was no better and no worse than any other
people. Yet God chose to reveal himself to the world
through Israel's history.

God's people were shattered

From the middle of the 8th century B.C. until the
beginning of the 6th century B.C. the political independence of Israel was destroyed bit by bit. After the
fall of the kingdom of Judah to the Babylonian army

in 586-587 B.C. Israel existed only as a religious minority in a province ruled by a series of different empires. Many Jews lived dispersed throughout various nations (the *Diaspora*). The priestly and ceremonial laws no longer regulated the public life of the nation. The land was possessed by others. It would not have been surprising if the people of Israel had lost their identity altogether during this time.

However, this was not the end of God's people. The destruction of the temple, the loss of the land, and the end of national independence had all been foretold by the prophets. They considered these things to be God's judgment on his disobedient people. The collapse of the nation was experienced as a disaster, but the faith of the people continued during the exile in Babylon and after the return:

Behold, the days are coming, says the Lord, when I will make a new covenant with the house of Israel and the house of Judah, not like the covenant which I made with their fathers when I took them by the hand to bring them out of the land of Egypt, my covenant which they broke, though I was their husband, says the Lord. But this is the covenant which I will make with the house of Israel after those days, says the Lord: I will put my law within them, and I will write it upon their hearts; and I will be their God, and they shall be my people. And no longer shall each man teach his neighbor and each his brother, saying, "Know the Lord," for they shall all know me, from the least of them to the greatest, says the Lord;

for I will forgive their iniquity, and I will remember their sin no more (Jer. 31:31-34).

God made a new beginning

"Has God rejected his people?" No, said Paul, and expressed his certainty with a reference to Ps. 94:14: "God has not rejected his people whom he foreknew" (Rom. 11:1-2). Instead God entered their history to reveal himself in a new way.

In Jesus of Nazareth God's covenant was not concluded, but extended. In Jesus the long-awaited reign of God promised by the prophets was at hand. Indeed, to encounter Jesus was to encounter God. This is the conviction Jesus aroused in his followers. That same experience is reflected throughout the New Testament. The Letter to the Colossians says Jesus is "the image of the invisible God" (Col. 1:15). The gospel of John declares, "No one has ever seen God; the only Son, who is in the bosom of the Father, he has made him known" (John 1:18).

Jesus called people to a radical trust in God and obedience to his will. He had a powerful impact on his friends and his enemies alike. Many followed him, but his message threatened the religious and political authorities. His ministry took him to an executioner's cross.

The cross is the focal point of the New Testament. It reveals God as one who participates with his people in their suffering. The God of the Bible forgives rebellious human beings, shows power in weakness, triumphs in defeat, and is glorified in the powerlessness of his servants.

Christian faith believes in a God who is both hidden and revealed. Martin Luther described the mysterious events of life as the acts of God in his "hiddenness." God can be experienced in the natural world, but his power there can be frightening as well as inspiring. Many people feel close to God on a beautiful day, but a tornado or earthquake brings them face to face with death and destruction.

If nature were our only clue to God, we would not be sure whether he is for us or against us. In Jesus Christ we know God is *for* us. Luther pointed to the Christ of Scripture as the only God we will ever know clearly. In the Bible we find a caring God who sacrifices himself for us, a "revealed God" who brings us the good news that he loves us more than we can imagine.

We can summarize what we have said so far in this way:

● The entire Bible talks about God, and has been written to reveal God to people. It does not indulge in abstract speculation about God. Instead, it tells the stories of people who have experienced God.

● God cannot be separated from the life and activity of Jesus. This has been asserted by the Christian faith from its very beginning.

5. How does the Bible describe God's will?

With the Ten Commandments the God of Israel placed his people under obligation. These commandments are referred to as the *Decalog,* or "ten words" God gave to Moses, written on two stone tablets (Exodus 20; 34). The number 10 does not have a special meaning in the Bible like the numbers 12, 7, or 3 do. It is a practical number. The Ten Commandments were intended for instruction. Children could count them off on their fingers to remember them. We call them "commandments," but that doesn't adequately describe them. They reveal the will of God for human beings, and they must be interpreted in a broad sense.

A great pledge is made at the very beginning of the Commandments: "I am the Lord your God, who brought you out of the land of Egypt, out of the house of bondage." With these words God laid the foundation for the covenant with his people. The one who gave the Commandments is the same one who delivered Israel from slavery in Egypt. He would continue to be their God.

The first three commandments stand apart from— and are basic to—all the others: "You shall have no other gods before me" (20:3). God wants the undivided love and obedience of his people. "You shall not take the name of the Lord your God in vain" (20:7). God wants to be called on in prayer and trust. "Remember the sabbath day, to keep it holy" (20:8).

God wants his people to take their rest and to praise and worship their Creator.

Commandments 4 through 10, sometimes called the "second table" of the law, protect the primary needs of human beings. Without observing these commandments, life in community would perish in chaos.

● The relationship between the generations should be determined by love and respect. Only in this way can a life of human dignity and togetherness be maintained.

● Human beings dare not take matters of life and death into their own hands, since it is all too easy for the strong to oppress the weak. Instead, our chief concern should be helping others who find themselves in need or difficulty.

● Marriage is an intentional and intimate partnership between a man and a woman. It should not be broken, because selfishness and insecurity easily lead to personal disaster. Instead, each of us ought to accept our life partners with all of their peculiarities and weaknesses, helping them to be the people God is creating them to be.

● Property that rightly belongs to another should not be infringed on. Instead, we ought to help each other use, develop, and manage all of our talents and all of the possessions God has entrusted to our care.

● False statements and loveless gossip should not be spoken about others. They result in suspicion, controversy, and hatred, poisoning people's lives. Instead, we should highlight the positive things about others, helping to create relationships of trust. Words, when spoken, take on an existence of their own, independent from their speaker. Therefore they are to be used with care.

● Envy and covetousness are particularly hazardous forms of selfish behavior, and should be excluded from every relationship. Instead, we ought to wish others every success from the bottom of our hearts and help them live out their lives in trust and fulfillment.

The Ten Commandments go far beyond legal regulation. The first three commandments make that quite clear. Therefore it is hard to base laws on them. Their intention goes far deeper than anything civil law can enforce, and they can only be fulfilled by those who fulfill them in their spirit as well as in their letter.

Unlike many of the rules and regulations found in the Old Testament, the Ten Commandments stand out as living statements of God's will in every age. They are aids in making human social life possible. They are God's gifts to his people of every time and every place. They have been rightly called the "Ten Great Freedoms." When human beings place their trust in God, the Commandments uphold and give shape to life.

Summary

● God has chosen to make himself known through human beings and the history of Israel.

● The Bible uses the language of metaphors. Its

stories, prayers, characters, and experiences speak to us in a deep and powerful way.

● The Bible bears witness that God is found by those who take the risk of trusting their lives to him.

● The God of the Bible forgives rebellious human beings, shows power in weakness, triumphs in defeat, and is glorified in the powerlessness of his servants.

● Christian faith believes in a God who is both hidden and revealed.

● The Ten Commandments stand out as living statements of God's will in every age.

For reflection

You will call upon me and come and pray to me, and I will hear you. You will seek me and find me; when you seek me with all your heart, I will be found by you. . . .

Jer. 29:12-14

Modern materialism is not very different from ancient polytheism, and the world has never worshipped as many idols as today. Cars, movie stars, political leaders, ideologies are the modern idols. The city streets and the highways are teeming with idols— the idols of commercial advertising and the idols of political propaganda, the smiling goddesses of fer-

tility and material abundance, quack medicines and
hygiene, the gods of beer, corn-flakes and denti-
frices; the faces of dictators and political bosses and
the somber deities of terror and war, of destruction
and death.

Ernesto Cardenal
To Live Is To Love
(Herder & Herder, 1972), p. 101

I asked the earth, and it said, "I am not he!" And all
things in it confessed the same. I asked the sea and
the deeps, and among living animals the things that
creep, and they answered, "We are not your God!
Seek you higher than us!" I asked the winds that
blow: and all the air, with the dwellers therein, said,
"Anaximenes was wrong. I am not God!" I asked the
heavens, the sun, the moon, and the stars: "We are
not the God whom you seek," said they. To all the
things that stand around the doors of my flesh I said,
"Tell me of my God! Although you are not he, tell
me something of him!" With a mighty voice they cried
out, "He made us!" My question was the gaze I turned
on them; the answer was their beauty.

Saint Augustine (354-430)
Confessions
(Doubleday, 1960), p. 234

I remember one day in the early springtime I was alone in the forest listening to the woodland sounds, and thinking only of one thing, the same of which I had constantly thought for two years—I was again seeking for a God. . . .

I began to retrace the process which had gone on within myself, the hundred times repeated discouragement and revival. I remembered that I had lived only when I believed in a God. As it was before, so it was now; I had only to know God, and I lived; I had only to forget Him, not to believe in Him, and I died. . . .

"What more, then, do I seek?" A voice seemed to cry within me, "This is He, He without whom there is no life. To know God and to live are one. God is life."

Leo Tolstoi (1828-1910)
Lift Up Your Eyes
(Julian, 1960), pp. 90-91

God does not die on the day when we cease to believe in a personal deity, but we die on the day when our lives cease to be illumined by the steady radiance, renewed daily, of a wonder, the source of which is beyond all reason.

Dag Hammarskjöld (1905-1961)

Markings
(Alfred A. Knopf, 1964), p. 56

Immortal, invisible, God only wise,
In light inaccessible hid from our eyes,
Most blessed, most glorious, the Ancient of Days,
Almighty, victorious, thy great name we praise!

W. Chalmers Smith (1824-1908)
Lutheran Book of Worship 526

5

Science and Creation

There are two different ways we human beings explore the world. We can isolate one small part of it and observe it closely. Such research gives us knowledge that helps us control nature. But we also need to construct a picture of the whole. When we attempt to do this, we do less observing, researching, and controlling than beholding, wondering, and adoring.

Both of these ways of exploring reality are important. They supplement each other. A geologist, for example, who has examined the various strata of a mountain can still be captivated by its majesty.

We live in a time when the first type of exploration —science—has accomplished amazing things. People are awed by what science and technology can do. But the second type of knowing—expressed in the arts, philosophy, and religion—is just as important.

1. How do the natural sciences understand the world?

According to "classical" physics, the world is made up of atoms suspended in space and time. These atoms consist of matter, which can produce forces as well as be influenced by forces. Each action has a cause and a reaction. According to this mechanical view, only things we can examine with scientific instruments are real.

In the 20th century, this simple framework has been made obsolete by physics itself. In his theory of relativity, Einstein pointed out that our usual concepts of space and time cannot explain the way many things in nature behave. Modern physics has had to completely rethink these concepts. Another blow to classical physics came with the first successful attempt to "split" an atom. In recent years scientists have been able to subdivide atoms into smaller and smaller "particles," with no end in sight. Some scientists now suggest that the whole distinction between "matter" and "forces" may no longer fit the evidence.

The discoveries and theories of 20th-century physics have shaken the scientific world and forced it to examine its basic principles more carefully. One of the facts modern scientists try to keep in mind is that there is no such thing as a totally objective observer. The result of every experiment is influenced by the subjectivity of the observer, the act of observation itself, and the instruments that are used. In addition, the answers scientists come up with depend entirely on the questions they ask.

Responsible scientists no longer talk about scientific "proof." Nothing can be "proven" scientifically. Instead, there are some theories that explain the known evidence better than other theories. All theories are subject to question and revision on the basis of new evidence. The goal of science is to construct a model of the universe that explains all the evidence in the most complete way possible.

Between 1600 and 1900, scientists generally thought the universe was infinite in space and time, with no beginning and no end. Today astronomers know that the galaxies are moving away from each other in a manner similar to an explosion. Most astrophysicists today assume the world began with an original explosion, or "big bang."

The chemical elements known today probably emerged in the early phases of cosmic development. They were formed by the extremely high pressures and temperatures of the initial explosion. Since that time the universe seems to have developed over a period of several dozen billion years. Astrophysicists calculate this figure by estimating the time it would have taken the galaxies to travel from one central spot to their present locations at their present rate of speed.

Scientists estimate that more than five billion years ago, a flat disc-like layer of gases with a concentrated central area emerged out of a gaseous cloud. Nuclear fusion began in the area of highest density and gave birth to our sun. Through a process of condensation, lasting some four billion years, other gaseous concentrations developed into the solid forms we know as the planets, including our earth. After the temperature of

SCIENCE AND CREATION 81

the earth had lowered sufficiently, steam finally condensed to water, and the seas were formed. Forces from within the earth and from the sun, air, and water led to the formation of land masses.

Current theories about the origin of living organisms say they appeared about three billion years ago in the sea, which by then had become salty. It has been suggested that all creatures are interrelated and form a hereditary unity, a huge family tree deeply rooted in the organic world. According to various theories, it has taken millions of years for higher, more differentiated, life forms to appear.

A remarkable interaction between the laws of nature and the appearance of new and novel life-forms seems to have led to the appearance of human beings. We should not take the scientific terms *evolution* or *development* in a mechanical sense. They describe the coming into being of something completely new, something that had never existed before. Most responsible scientists are content to describe the history of life on earth, without concluding whether or not a Creator was at work in that history.

2. What does the Bible say about the origin of the world?

The creation accounts

"In the beginning God created the heavens and the earth" (Gen. 1:1). This sentence stands at the beginning of the Bible, but the understanding it expresses was not simply assumed from the beginning. Faith in God as the Creator developed as the people of Israel reflected on God's saving acts in their history. The central point of Israel's creed was not a statement about the creation of the world, but the story of the deliverance from Egypt. The conclusion that God is sovereign over all things was a direct consequence of God's command, "You shall have no other gods before me" (Exod. 20:3). The resulting confession was, God is not only the Lord of the people of Israel, not merely the God of Abraham, Isaac, and Jacob, but this same God is also the Lord of the whole world, Creator of the universe.

The Bible speaks of creation in more than one place and in a variety of ways. Some of the later descriptions emphasize the role of God's word in creating the world. The older accounts speak of creation as a formation, establishment, or separation. Nowhere does the Bible fully explain the process of creation. Each description comes from a different historical setting, yet all of them focus their attention on the Creator.

In Genesis 1, which was actually written later than Genesis 2, there are already clues that foreshadow scientific investigation of the world and human beings. Genesis 1 implies that the affirmation of God as Creator does not exclude scientific research into the world's origin. The fact that two different stories of creation (Genesis 1 and Genesis 2) were allowed to stand together in the Bible suggests that the question of *how* God created the world is not a vital issue for faith. The Bible does not require us to have a particular theory of creation. Instead, it gives us the freedom to investigate the world's origin, always giving glory to the Creator behind it all.

None of the biblical creation stories are historical reports. Instead, they talk about the relationship between God, human beings, and the world, using the language of symbols and images. They use the thought-forms and knowledge of their times to say some important things about God, his people, and his world.

The account in Genesis 1 organizes creation around seven days. The world is presented as having developed in a series of time periods. The "rest" prescribed for the seventh day suggests the world is moving toward a particular goal.

Genesis 1 describes the creative action of God with a Hebrew word ("created" in v. 1) that is used only in connection with God, never with human beings. In this way it underscores the unique nature of God's creativity. God called the world into being through his word. This means:

● The world did not emerge from God's own being; the Creator and the creation are sharply distinguished.

● God's word is a creative force: "For he spoke, and it came to pass; he commanded, and it stood fast" (Ps. 33:9). The world exists because God wills it to exist.

● Because of God's word, the world has purpose

and order. The world reflects the intentions of its Creator.

Everything that has been created is constantly threatened by a return to chaos, the possibility of disintegrating into nothingness. That is the significance of the words, "without form and void," and "the face of the deep." The world is in constant need of God's creative activity in order to stay in existence.

God created the framework for everything else that takes place in three striking acts of separation. Time began with the separation of light from darkness. Space originated with the separation of the heavens from the earth (vertical), and the seas from the dry land (horizontal).

The sun, moon, and stars do not make their appearance in the story until the fourth day. The narrator deliberately put them in fourth place, because he lived at a time when people worshiped these heavenly bodies. It was important to emphasize that they are not gods. They were created to perform a particular function: to provide light.

Plants and animals were each created according to their kind. Here we can detect an interest in classifying living beings into different categories. This early biology reflects the beginnings of science in the ancient world.

The narrator tells us that God made a definite decision to create human beings, underscoring the im-

portance of human life in creation. Unlike the older
creation account in Genesis 2, no attempt is made here
to describe the process involved. This is the writer's
way of preserving the mystery of creation. The distinction between men and women is not mentioned.
God blesses the fertility of the human race, and tells
people to fill the earth, to subdue or manage it, and to
have dominion over every living thing.

Some people have blamed this command for an un-
inhibited exploitation of nature and the destruction of
our environment. We must understand that the narrator of this story emphasized "dominion" as an expression of our creation in God's image. Human beings are to relate to nature in the same way God
relates to them. We are not just given control *over*
nature, but also responsibility *for* nature.

The statement, "God created man in his own image"
says something about the relationship between God
and human beings as well as the relationship between
people and the world:

● God created human beings as companions, partners he could talk to and who could respond to him.
Our partnership with God is the foundation for our
dignity as persons and our human rights.

● In ancient times certain images were designated
to represent kings. This text may be alluding to the
fact that we are "living images" authorized to represent God's lordship over the earth.

"God saw everything that he had made, and behold, it was very good" (Gen. 1:31). When we look at the world we also see cruelty and senselessness. This makes God's statement difficult to understand. What it means is that in God's eyes creation is an orderly and coherent whole. Creation is good because it left God's hands in good condition and is still capable of becoming what God intends it to be. God will bring his creation to a good conclusion, despite every evil that has entered it through human beings. Its original goal will be accomplished. So we have a reason to rejoice in God's good creation, despite suffering, for God is still working through it for good.

The Genesis 1 account concludes with God resting on the seventh day. To the passing of days, God adds one very special day as a gift to human beings. This is a clear reference to the Sabbath day, which was a day of rest. At the same time, the seventh day points toward a future when all human works and deeds will be brought to fulfillment.

The older creation account in Genesis 2 deals mostly with the creation of human beings. It forms a unit with the story of disobedience in Genesis 3. By placing the two stories together, the writer expresses the human predicament: we have been created good by God, and yet we have the possibility of opposing God.

The theme of creation from the earth was a common one in the ancient world. The narrator does not intend it in a literal sense. Still, he uses it to make a point: human beings are created by God, yet are

made of earthly elements. God breathes into our
nostrils the breath of life and we become living beings. No distinction between body and soul was intended by this image. Instead, the human person is
seen as a living totality. God gives life, but he can
also take it back. When he does, those from whom he
takes it return to the earth from which they came. The
Hebrew word *adam* is not a personal name. It means
"humanity," and is a pun on the word *adamah,*
"earth." Adam and Eve, though personified as individuals in the story, are not necessarily individual persons, but representatives of humanity.

In the Garden of Eden work is portrayed as a valid
part of human life. The earth is meant to be tilled and
protected by its human inhabitants. The statement,
"It is not good that man should be alone," expresses
the truth that human beings find fulfillment only in
community. By using an ancient story about the creation of animals, the biblical writer points out that the
man himself is to determine which partner suits him
best. The meaning is clear: community is possible
only when persons commit themselves to each other
freely and responsibly. In naming the animals, the
man orders the world with the assistance of language.

The creation of a woman from the rib of the man,
like the creation of the man from the earth, is not
meant to be taken literally. The narrator is making
the point that human beings can enter relationships
that have no parallel in the animal world. The man
has a mate fit for him: "This at last is bone of my bones

and flesh of my flesh." The compelling power of love between women and men is established in creation.

The meaning of creation

In everything it says about creation, the Bible underscores the relationship between God and his world, between human beings and all other creatures, between individuals and the whole. Human beings are therefore related both to the Creator and to everything else God has created. The Bible is filled with the praises of creation given to its marvelous Creator.

Because God created the world, all things are interconnected. Human beings are dependent on the rest of creation. In recent years the possibilities for mastering the earth and radically altering nature have multiplied. We are coming perilously close to threatening the foundation for our own existence. It is essential that we come to a new appreciation of our dependence on the world God has created for us.

Our world is constantly changing. But this will not continue forever. The world remains in the hands of its Creator. It had a beginning and it will have an end. The story of the flood in Genesis 6–9 is complementary to the creation stories. God's will brought the world into being; that same will can also bring it to an end. At the conclusion of the flood story, God promises, "While the earth remains, seedtime and harvest, cold and heat, summer and winter, day and night, shall not cease" (8:22). Today the threat of worldwide destruction at human hands is more dangerous than the threat of natural disasters. God's command "to till" the garden and to "keep it" (2:15) remains in force. Today this command can no longer be restricted to personal life: it can only be obeyed by an assumption of responsibility for the whole earth by all human beings. If we shun this responsibility, God can give us over to the inevitable result of our own race toward self-destruction.

The Bible begins with the origin of the world and human beings. It ends in an equally universal way. Both the Old and New Testaments end in apocalyptic visions of how God will bring human history to a conclusion. When the mission of God's people reaches its appointed goal, history will have achieved its final destiny. Only in the end will the meaning of the whole creation become clear.

3. What is the relationship between science and the biblical accounts of creation?

Are faith and science in opposition?

To this day, the opinion is rather widespread that faith and science are in opposition. Both religious critics and Christians have often made the same mistake. They have failed to take into account the limits of one viewpoint and the contributions another viewpoint can make. Some people expect answers for all of life's questions from science. Others assume that the Bible is a scientific textbook.

The Bible, however, does not try to provide new

scientific insights. Instead, it states that the world did not just happen. It had a Creator who called it into being and who sustains it; it has purpose and a goal. As we have already seen, the Bible uses many different images and metaphors to express these thoughts. In fact, the Genesis 1 account of creation uses the scientific insights of its time as it points to the Creator. In doing this, it does not bind future generations to ancient scientific views. Instead it encourages *us* to study the world's origins by using the science of our own time.

The certainty that God has created, sustains, loves, and directs the world toward its goal does not find its source in science. It comes from an encounter with God and is experienced by faith. Contemporary scientific views of the world are the backdrop, the setting for our affirmation of faith.

The Bible tells us about experiences people have had with God so that we might have similar experiences. Generally speaking, we meet God through other individuals, events, or circumstances; that is, through earthly things. Science is able to describe the physical circumstances of these events, but it cannot interpret what they mean to those who experience them.

Each of the natural sciences has a precisely defined field of investigation and its own methods and procedures. Experiments are devised so that the situation can be as controlled as possible, and the observers as objective as possible. By contrast, experiences of God cannot be controlled. Further, it is impossible to experience God and remain coldly analytical. The whole person is involved—not only the mind but also the emotions and the will. Experiences of God always have subjective elements, and therefore science can never describe them in all their fullness.

Opposition between faith and science always surfaces when one or the other, or both, step beyond their own boundaries and assume that their way of viewing reality is the only way. When both science and faith remain true to their proper tasks, there can be no irreconcilable differences. Christian faith affirms the integrity of the natural sciences. It stands opposed to the absolutizing of any single point of view, and supports an open-ended understanding of the world.

Are faith and science unrelated?

Many people have concluded, on the basis of these insights, that faith and science are separate domains. Neither has the right to meddle in the affairs of the other. Faith is concerned with the relationship between human beings and God. Science is concerned with exploring the world. They are seen as two distinct ways of observing reality. According to this view, there can be no conflict between them.

Sometimes Christians state their beliefs without regard for what science has learned. Scientists sometimes act as though faith has nothing to say about what they do with their knowledge. Such attitudes exaggerate the separation between faith and science. These are two different ways to view the world, but they are talking about the same world. It is important that faith and science pay attention to each other.

Are faith and science complementary?

Faith and science exist in the same world. A Christian can be a scientist and a scientist can be a Christian. The biblical creation stories accept the scientific findings of their day and interpret them. Today Christians must not ignore the natural sciences. Much can be learned from them. Biologists talk about the evolution of life on earth. Isn't it possible that God could have directed such an evolution? Genesis itself affirms the orderliness of creation in all its variety and stages. It is not necessary to throw out modern science in order to make room for God. God does not act only in the places where science cannot observe what he does. The origin of the world and the development of life are, in their totality, the creative work of God.

Faith and science complement each other. Together they provide us not only with an understanding of reality, but also help us to deal with it. Science develops technology and demonstrates how it can change our world. Science tells us what we *can* do. But what tells us who we are and what we *should* do? Only the God who created us and loves us can tell us these things.

Summary

- All scientific theories are subject to question and revision on the basis of new evidence.

- Faith in God as the Creator developed as the people of Israel reflected on God's saving acts in their history.

- The biblical creation stories talk about the relationship between God, human beings, and the world.

- Human beings belong to creation; they also belong to God.

- God created the world to be good. The world remains in the hands of its Creator.

- Faith and natural science complement each other.

For reflection

Hallelujah!
Praise the Lord from the heavens;
praise him in the heights.
Praise him, all you angels of his;
praise him, all his host.
Praise him, sun and moon;
praise him, all you shining stars.
Praise him, heaven of heavens,
and you waters above the heavens.
Let them praise the name of the Lord;
for he commanded, and they were created.

SCIENCE AND CREATION 95

He made them stand fast forever and ever;
he gave them a law which shall not pass away.

Ps. 148:1-6

This is my Father's world,
And to my list'ning ears
All nature sings, and round me rings
The music of the spheres.
This is my Father's world;
I rest me in the thought
Of rocks and trees, of skies and seas;
His hand the wonders wrought.

Maltbie D. Babcock (1858-1901)
Lutheran Book of Worship 554

Nature is like the shadow of God, a reflection of
His beauty and His splendor. The blue of the placid
lake mirrors this divine splendor. God's fingerprints
are impressed on every particle of matter. In every
atom an image of the Trinity is enshrined, a faint re-
semblance of the Triune God. And this, Oh Lord, is
why your creation fills us with rapturous enthusiasm.

My entire body, too, has been made to love God.
Each of its cells is a hymn to the Creator and a con-
tinuous declaration of love. As the kingfisher has

been made to catch fish . . . so man has been made for the contemplation and love of God.

Ernesto Cardenal
To Live Is To Love
(Herder & Herder, 1972), pp. 26-27

All things were named—all but man himself, then the sleep fell upon the Adam, and in that first sleep he strove to utter his name, and as he strove he was divided and woke to find humanity doubled. The name of mankind was in neither voice but in both; the knowledge of the name and its utterance was in the perpetual interchange of love.

Charles Williams (1886-1945)
The Place of the Lion
(Eerdmans, 1976), p. 191

The creation story contains God's commission to man: Subdue the earth. In every ancient religion the earth is holy. She is worshipped as the earth mother. This commission has something horrifying about it. Dominate the earth mother! This is too bold. This is blasphemy. God himself commands man to destroy the ancient world, to shatter its deepest piety and throw out its most basic superstition. The God of the Bible himself commands man to overthrow the throne on which he sits. And this means that science is in no way the enemy of religion but its historical successor.

Dorothee Sölle
The Truth Is Concrete
(Burns and Oates, 1969), pp. 13-14

Lord of lords,
Creator of all things,
God over all gods,
God of sun and rain,
You created the earth with a thought
and us
with Your breath. . . .
Lord,
the yam is fat like meat,
the cassava melts on the tongue,
oranges burst in their peels,
dazzling and bright.
Lord,
nature gives thanks.
Your creatures give thanks. . . .

African prayer, Fritz Pawelzik, ed.
I Sing Your Praise All the Day Long
(© 1967 by Friendship Press), p. 40
Used by permission.

6

Christian Faith and Non-Christian Religions

The methods of science and the insights of faith do not exhaust the perspectives by which people understand the world. There are many different ways of looking at the world, many different "world views." Most people in the world today are not Christian in faith or commitment, but look at the world through the eyes of some other religion (such as Hinduism) or world view (such as Marxism).

The question of how Christian faith differs from other religions is especially important for our time. Not only are Asian religions—primarily those of India —today engaging in strong missionary activity within the western world, but we now live in a kind of "free market" of religious ideas. Christians can no longer live a secluded existence. The relationship between Christian faith and non-Christian religions urgently needs to be addressed.

1. What are the major world religions?

There are only a handful of religions that can be said to be "world" religions in the sense that they have had a broad and fundamental impact on more than one civilization. These religions come out of three different cultures, and it is helpful to distinguish them on that basis.

Best known to us are those that come from the ancient Near East: Judaism, Christianity, and Islam. All three were influenced by Graeco-Roman civilization. In these faiths the overriding concern is the relationship of human beings to God. If God is rightly known, trusted, and believed in, then the whole of life—including one's self and the world—is put into proper perspective.

Next most familiar are the religions that began in India, especially Hinduism and Buddhism. Though they have basic differences, the important view these religions share is that everything depends on a correct understanding and experience of one's self.

Less well-known than these are the religions of the Chinese tradition. The most important are Confucianism and Taoism. While very different from each other, both hold our experience of the world here and now to be most significant.

Judaism

Modern Judaism has a close relationship to the Jewish faith that existed at the time of Jesus. Together with Christianity it grew out of the Hebrew experience of God as Creator of the world, Redeemer of his people, and initiator of a covenant relationship.

The central confession of Judaism is, "Hear, O

Israel, the Lord our God, the Lord is one Lord"
(Deut. 6:4). There is one God and he has chosen
Israel to be a holy nation. Through Israel he intends
to reveal his love, compassion, law, and justice to the
world.

Judaism understands all of life to be under the rule
and blessing of God. The Old Testament law or *Torah*
(the first five books of the Bible) is concerned with
every aspect of life: personal, social, and economic.
All people are to act in harmony with God's righteousness and give glory to his name. Within the social
realm there is to be justice, truth, and peace. The
basic standard of all social relationships is "You shall
love your neighbor as yourself" (Lev. 19:18).

After the destruction of Jerusalem in 70 A.D.,
Judaism went through a period of change and adjust-
ment. It was no longer possible to continue the rituals
of priestly service and sacrifice in the Temple. The
rabbis (teachers) in the scattered Jewish communities continued to discuss and interpret the Torah.
They believed God had revealed many things to
Moses in addition to the Torah that aided its understanding and application to life. These oral traditions
were thought to have been preserved and transmitted
down through the generations. In centers of Jewish
life such as Palestine and Babylonia the rabbis com-
piled and codified these traditions. Between 300 and
500 A.D. they were put into writing in a large collection known as the *Talmud*. Talmudic literature has

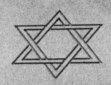

HAPPY ARE
THEY THAT
DWELL IN
THY HOUSE

אשרי יושבי
ביתך

provided detailed commentary on the Torah to help Jewish communities adapt the biblical traditions to new and different social situations.

The main centers of Jewish religious life are the home and the synagogue. In these places God is worshiped, Torah and the rest of the Hebrew Bible are studied, and the ancient traditions of Judaism are kept alive. There are various expressions of Judaism in the modern world. Some of the more widespread forms of Jewish faith are the following:

● *Orthodox Judaism* maintains the traditional view that all of life must conform to the detailed regulations of Torah and Talmud;

● *Conservative Judaism* emphasizes the role of the written tradition, yet allows for some latitude in its interpretation and practice today;

● *Reform Judaism* believes the principles of Judaism are of primary importance, and that the traditional rituals and regulations must be adapted to changing circumstances.

In addition to the different religious interpretations of Judaism, there is also the modern movement known as Zionism. Zionism emphasizes the role of the land of Israel in the life of the Jewish people. Zionism is primarily a political and nationalistic movement, not tied to one particular interpretation of Jewish religion, yet it is often related to Jewish faith.

Islam

Islam is the most recent of the major world religions, tracing its beginnings to the seventh century A.D. and the utterances of Muhammad. A reformer of the ancient Arabian folk religion, Muhammad was greatly influenced by both Judaism and Christianity. He taught a distinctive understanding of the unity and kingship of God. His words were written in the Quran, the Muslim Scriptures.

The fundamental confession of Muslims is, "There is no God but God (no Allah but Allah), and Muhammad is his prophet." *Islam* means "submission," and this submission to God is a matter of great importance. People were created by God to be his representatives in the world, and it is necessary for them to know his will and to do it. In order to persuade people to submit to the will of God, Muhammad preached both the judgment of God on the wicked and the resurrection to eternal life of the obedient.

For Islam, submission to God includes all of life. Not only religious life, but also social, economic, political, and cultural life must come under his rule. Because of this emphasis Islam has seen repeated attempts to completely reform and reorient society. Such efforts often show a harsh rejection of all values and practices that deviate from the norms of Islam.

There are two main divisions within Islam. Most Muslims are part of *Sunni* Islam. The largest minority belong to *Shiite* Islam. The differences between these movements date from a dispute over the office of *caliph,* the successor to Muhammad. The Sunnis hold that the Caliph can be elected by a council from the tribe of Muhammad, while the Shiites believe the post is limited to descendants of Muhammad's son-in-law Ali.

Islam showed itself from the outset to be an aggressive missionary movement. Certain key themes have enabled it to find a home in different cultures and still retain its unity. Important among these are the "five pillars" or chief duties of Muslims: confession of faith in God (Allah), prayer five times each day, the giving of alms, fasting during certain days of the year, and making a pilgrimage to Mecca.

Hinduism

Hinduism and Buddhism share much in common. Existence is seen as an endless cycle of becoming and passing away. In the course of this endless cycle innumerable worlds arise and decay, together with all the beings that inhabit them. In this process the sum total or "fruit" of each life becomes a shaping force *(karma)* that determines the destiny of the next birth. Each new existence ("reincarnation") lives out of the previous karma and shapes the karma for the next birth. The wheel of new becomings turns endlessly, without rest and without purpose. The only possible escape is through liberation from this wheel. Hinduism and Buddhism each describe different ways of liberation.

Hinduism emphasizes that the self is not to be iden-

tified with the bodily self. The real self is immaterial, unchangeable, and eternal, and only realizes its true nature when it experiences its union with the "absolute self," the one self that pervades all things. "Salvation" comes when this unity is fully realized, when an individual realizes that he or she is identical with the one universal "self."

Hinduism offers many paths or methods for achieving this sense of oneness. These include intuitive insight, yoga and meditation, ritual purification, and devotion to a particular deity.

Buddhism

Siddhartha Gautama, born about 560 B.C. in India, was overcome by the endless suffering all creatures were doomed to undergo. He sought enlightenment and deliverance through the teachings and practices of the leading holy men of his day. Finally, convinced that the answer lay elsewhere, he waited in meditation. Enlightenment came, and he became the "Buddha" ("enlightened one").

In the overpowering light of his experience of enlightenment, Buddha saw these truths: everything that exists suffers; suffering results from self-centered entanglements with life; suffering can be resolved only by eliminating the illusion that an individual self really exists and eliminating all attachments to the world. These three truths were supplemented by a fourth that spelled out the path of enlightenment.

This path included moral training, practice in meditation, and the cultivation of wisdom and insight.

The Buddhist experience of *Nirvana* (freedom from self) is similar to the Hindu experience of *Brahman* (discovery of the true self), and often the ways of speaking overlap. The crucial difference is that Buddhism denies the ultimate existence of an individual self. It believes all pain and disillusionment comes from the belief that we actually are individuals. With bliss and insight the realization comes that we are part of a transcendent unity and are not individual selves.

Confucianism and Taoism

Confucians understand the world as essentially a moral reality. Taoists see it as a natural reality. It can be debated whether these two movements are actually religions, but their concerns are so all-embracing that they are usually treated along with the other major religions.

Confucius lived in the fifth century B.C. during a time of political and moral upheaval. He tried to bring about a truly moral order in society. He felt himself compelled by "heaven" to carry out his teaching mission, and he looked to wise rulers of the past for inspiration. He saw morality in the context of human relationships. A child's appropriate attitude toward his or her parents was considered the starting point for all morality.

Confucius believed that if correct relationships existed among people, then families, society, and the state would all be harmoniously ordered. They would resonate with the moral order in the universe. This harmony is nurtured and expressed in many ways, but especially through the veneration of one's ancestors.

Taoism is a term that includes many traditions, including some explicitly religious ones. All the different traditions received their basic inspiration from a philosophy that emphasizes the rhythms and transformations of nature. Human liberation is not achieved by escape from these processes (as in Buddhism) or by interfering with them through social and moral manipulation (as in Confucianism), but by yielding to them. We must experience our own nature as part of these rhythms.

2. How does the Christian view of God differ?

Differences from Asian religions

The basic difference between the Semitic faiths growing out of the ancient Near East and the Asian faiths becomes clear when we speak of creation. Jews, Christians, and Muslims all believe in God's creative action, an action not to be undone by anyone. God established a relationship with a world that is quite distinct from his own self.

Hindus, Buddhists, and Taoists do not acknowledge God's creation of the world. Instead, the world, the self, and God (or the "absolute self") are all different expressions of the same basic reality. The relation between individuals and God is not a personal one, but an impersonal one, either mystical or moral.

Religions of Asia understand life to be a process of absorption into a greater whole, often conceived in impersonal terms. The religions that trace their ancestry to the people of Israel all emphasize life as an experience of encountering a personal God, the Creator and Redeemer.

Differences from Islam

The key difference betwen the Judeo-Christian tradition and Islam concerns the understanding of how and in what way God cares for his creation. For Muslims, human beings are God's representatives on earth. God gives clear commands as to what must be done, and our duty is to obey. If we make a mistake, it is possible that he will forgive us. Never, however, does God (Allah) commit himself to his creation. He does not bind himself with a covenant. Creation is never permitted to infringe on his sovereignty, freedom, and unity. Only God's *will* is known by human beings, never God himself.

According to the Judeo-Christian tradition, this is not an adequate understanding. God not only creates the world, he also cares for it. In his freedom he chooses to involve himself in his world. God can be pictured as weeping, pleading, speaking angrily, even suffering grief as though he were in childbirth—all symbols of his great love for what he has made.

Differences from Judaism

There is no other faith with which Christian faith has so much in common as Judaism. The assumptions about God are the same, as are the understandings of revelation and faith, and also many elements of tradition and practice. The Hebrew Bible is the Christian Old Testament. There is also a great and sad common history of Christians and Jews living together.

Although there are many differences between Christian faith and Judaism, the most basic doctrinal difference is the understanding of Jesus. From its earliest beginnings, the Christian faith confessed Jesus of Nazareth to be the promised king of Israel. Christians saw him as the fulfillment of God's Old Testament promises. Many Jews could not share this faith. Further, the idea of worshiping a human being is foreign to the Old Testament. The Christian identification of Jesus with God seems blasphemous.

Jews have serious grounds on which to question the Christian claim that God's promises have been fulfilled in Jesus. If so, they say, how can all the centuries of anti-Semitism be explained, let alone the Holocaust? In our time Christians and Jews are only beginning the long process of conversation and increased mutual understanding. Faithfulness to the Old Testament tradition and the God in whom both traditions confess their faith requires that the process of dialog, repentance, and forgiveness continue.

Summary

- Modern Judaism has a close relationship to the Jewish faith that existed at the time of Jesus.
- The fundamental confession of all Muslims is, "There is no God but God, and Muhammad is his prophet."
- Both Hinduism and Buddhism see existence as an endless cycle of becoming and passing away.
- Confucians understand the world as essentially a moral reality. Taoists see it as a natural reality.
- There is no other faith with which Christian faith has so much in common as Judaism.
- The most basic doctrinal difference between Christians and Jews concerns their understandings of Jesus.

For reflection

Men of Athens, I perceive that in every way you are very religious. For as I passed along, and observed the objects of your worship, I found also an altar with this inscription, "To an unknown god". . . . The times of ignorance God overlooked, but now he commands all men everywhere to repent.

Acts 17:22-23, 30

Several of the ancient religions of the world have entered into a missionary phase of their existence.

In the West truth is singular. There has been a sense of theological rightness, resting on the belief that in the Word of God Christians possess the single truth. The new religious consciousness leans instead to the Asian conception of truth. In India the truth has many names. There are as many paths to the truth as there are seekers on the way. In a very tolerant way, Hindus and Buddhists believe everyone has a part of the truth, however rudimentary, and should be encouraged to follow that truth in confidence that it will lead finally to higher truth.

Howard A. Wilson
Invasion from the East
(Augsburg, 1978), pp. 33-34

They will have their questions to ask of us, and some of these may prove highly embarrassing. . . . But, if it is our incomparable privilege to stand within the truth, we shall have everything to gain and nothing to lose by exposing ourselves to questioning. The questions should help to elucidate our faith, to open up aspects of it that were previously hidden from us, perhaps to rid us of some illusions, and in the end to strengthen our hold on that which, or rather him whom, we have believed.

Stephen Neill
Christian Faith and Other Faiths
(Oxford, 1970), pp. 6-7

The Holocaust is the unfinished business of the
Christian churches, the running sore unattended by its
leaders and weakening to its constituents. . . . More
than anything else that has happened since the fourth
century, it has called into question the integrity of the
Christian people. . . .

Franklin H. Littell
The Crucifixion of the Jews
(Harper & Row, 1975), p. 129

The SS seemed more preoccupied, more disturbed
than usual. To hang a young boy in front of thousands of spectators was no light matter. . . .
"Where is God? Where is He?" someone behind me
asked.
At a sign from the head of the camp, the three
chairs tipped over. . . .
For more than half an hour he stayed there, struggling between life and death, dying in slow agony
under our eyes. And we had to look him full in the
face. . . .
Behind me, I heard the same man asking:
"Where is God now?"
And I heard a voice within me answer him:
"Where is He? Here he is—He is hanging here on this
gallows. . . ."

Elie Wiesel
Night
(Hill & Wang, 1969), p. 44

God, whose almighty word
Chaos and darkness heard
And took their flight:
Hear us, we humbly pray,
And where the Gospel day
Sheds not its glorious ray,
Let there be light!

John Marriott (1780-1825)
Lutheran Book of Worship 400

Part Three

What Is Sin?

If only it were all so simple! If only there were evil people somewhere insidiously committing evil deeds, and it were necessary only to separate them from the rest of us and destroy them. But the line dividing good and evil cuts through the heart of every human being. And who is willing to destroy a piece of his own heart?

During the life of any heart this line keeps changing place; sometimes it is squeezed one way by exuberant evil and sometimes it shifts to allow enough space for good to flourish. One and the same human being is, at various ages, under various circumstances, a totally different human being. At times he is close to being a devil, at times to sainthood. But his name doesn't change, and to that name we ascribe the whole lot, good and evil.

Socrates taught us, "Know thyself!"

Confronted by the pit into which we are about to toss those who have done us harm, we halt, stricken dumb: it is after all only because of the way things worked out that they were the executioners and we weren't . . . .

From good to evil is one quaver, says the proverb.

And correspondingly, from evil to good.

Aleksandr I. Solzhenitsyn
The Gulag Archipelago
(Harper & Row, 1973), p. 168

7

Illusion and Reality

How do we see ourselves? What kind of a world have we fashioned out of God's created order? It is not hard to discover the image we would *like* to have of ourselves. Advertisers know how to appeal to our dreams and fantasies, and they picture us in an impressive way: successful, carefree, mobile—masters of technology. They offer us an amazing array of products to capture our fancy and make life more enjoyable.

The message of advertising is that technology has taken us beyond good and evil. The answer to every human need can be found on the shelf of a store. All we need to do to solve our problems is use our affluence wisely and spread its benefits to others.

Unfortunately, the realities of our world do not conform to this illusion. Modern society is being severely threatened by forces pulling it apart at the seams. Many of our problems have reached crisis proportions, and technology has not provided the answers we need.

1. Chemical dependency

One of the signs of the failure of modern society is the number of people who have little idea of who they are or where they are headed. Our culture no longer gives clear answers to these questions, and people look for their own answers wherever they think they can find them. Some lose themselves in constant noise or visual stimulation; others look for fulfillment through temporary sexual relationships; still others use chemicals such as tranquilizers, alcohol, or illegal drugs. Those who abuse chemicals often become emotionally or physically dependent on them.

The problem of chemical dependency is not new. Alcoholism and drug abuse have existed in some cultures for thousands of years. Today, however, the problem is growing at a frightening rate. Few families have been left untouched by chemical dependency.

The psychological causes of this disease are still unclear. Medical science has not yet determined why some people become dependent more easily than others. Significant advances, however, have been made in the *treatment* of dependency. Doctors—and even courts—now recognize that chemicals can exert an almost demonic power over a person's behavior, thoughts, and feelings. It is necessary to remove the toxic substances from the body before a dependent

person can fully cooperate in the long process of re-
covery.

Chemical dependency is a serious and widespread
illness that leaves no social class unaffected. Only a
small percentage of those who are chemically dependent conform to the "skid row" image. The great
majority can be found throughout society, trying to
function as well as they can.

Dependency disrupts behavior, poisons relationships, and ruins the health of its victims. It is a serious
symptom of a society that does not live up to its
happy and carefree image of itself.

2. Violence

There is hardly any way in which evil is experienced with more immediate suffering than through
violence: murder, rape, kidnapping, revolutionary violence, terrorism, repression, torture, and war. Violence
has a way of becoming intensified through provoca-
tion and retaliation. Violence often occurs when individuals, groups, or nations lose confidence in other
means of accomplishing their goals. The results of
poverty and hopelessness may be violent crime or
rioting. The breakdown of the vehicles for social
change may invite terrorism or revolution. Loss of
order and stability may lead to governmental repression. Today violence in all its forms is an increasing
threat to the very fabric of civilization.

Power can become intoxicating. The driver of a car senses it when he or she pushes the gas pedal to the floor and leaves everyone else behind. There is something very appealing about having power and using it. But notice how quickly power can turn into aggression when a driver finds a slow-moving vehicle blocking the passing lane! The possession of superior power can make us blind toward others.

Life in a community cannot be regulated without the exercise of power. Power can be used legitimately by those who are accountable to society and use it to build up instead of to destroy. All those in positions of authority have a responsibility to protect the rights of others. Sometimes the carrying out of this responsibility requires the use of force. A police officer who arrests a violent criminal is protecting the rights of everyone else in the community.

This leads to the question of war. Wars cause immense suffering and misery. Not only is there a terrible loss of life, but also an ugly aftermath: illness, hunger, theft, brutality, desolation, and the breakdown of morality and social structures. The Augsburg Confession refers to "just wars," wars in which there is a legitimate government, a legitimate reason, a just purpose, and a proper manner of engagement (Article 16). With the appearance of weapons of mass destruction in the 20th century, it has become questionable whether it is still possible to wage a "just war." Little or no distinction is made anymore between soldiers and civilians, even in small-scale conflicts. And the

only possible outcome of a war between the super-powers would be worldwide destruction and the death of hundreds of millions (if not billions) of people. It must be a high priority of every person to help prevent such a war.

One of the ironies of modern military strategy is the concept that we must be prepared to destroy the world in order to prevent its destruction. We prepare for "defense" instead of war. A soldier in such an army could be said to be pursuing peace, even though appearances are just the opposite. On the other hand, those who call such reasoning madness and refuse to bear arms must be respected. It is only a very limited kind of security that can be found in the threat of a nuclear war.

3. Environmental contamination

During the past quarter of a century the contamination of our environment with dangerous and even lethal materials has grown to alarming proportions. The seriousness of the problem can no longer be avoided. The joy of technical progress has been replaced by a deep fear of its consequences.

Toward the end of the 1960s various countries began impressive programs designed to protect the environment. To date some progress has been made, but we now realize that an absolute commitment to the environment is not compatible with a commitment to economic growth. Decision making in this area is

made even more difficult by the recognition that less-developed countries must continue the process of industrialization if they are to meet the pressing needs of their populations.

We are living on an increasingly poisoned and over-populated planet. It is questionable whether techno-logical solutions will be able to deal with the problem. They may only add to the disruption of an already endangered ecological system.

At the root of our problem is the change in values that has taken place in the western world over the last three hundred years. Human beings have come to be valued more for what they achieve or possess than for who they are. The consequences of an ever-increasing greed for possessions have been disastrous: the mass pillage of the planet, the thoughtless use of hazardous chemicals, the dispensing of drugs before their long-range effects are known. Both "capitalist" and "socialist" economic systems have contributed to the problem. Representatives from less-developed nations point out that a resident of the United States, Europe, or the Soviet Union places many times more stress on the planet's resources than a resident of Asia, Africa, or Latin America.

Summary

● Chemical dependency is a serious and wide-spread illness that leaves no social class unaffected.

● Violence often occurs when individuals, groups,

or nations lose confidence in other means of accomplishing their goals.

● Power can be used legitimately by those who are accountable to society and use it to build up instead of to destroy.

● With the appearance of weapons of mass destruction in the 20th century, it has become questionable whether it is still possible to wage a "just war."

● During the past quarter of a century the contamination of our environment with dangerous and even lethal materials has taken on alarming proportions.

● The joy of technical progress has been replaced by a deep fear of its consequences.

For reflection

Let us conduct ourselves becomingly as in the day, not in reveling and drunkenness, not in debauchery and licentiousness, not in quarreling and jealousy. But put on the Lord Jesus Christ, and make no provision for the flesh, to gratify its desires.

Rom. 13:13-14

And he sent messengers ahead of him, who went and entered a village of the Samaritans, to make ready for him; but the people would not receive him, because his face was set toward Jerusalem. And when his disciples James and John saw it, they said, "Lord, do you want us to bid fire come down from heaven and consume them?" But he turned and rebuked them. And they went on to another village.

Luke 9:51-56

The Lord God took the man and put him in the garden of Eden to till it and keep it.

Gen. 2:15

We travel together, passengers on a little spaceship, dependent on its vulnerable reserves of air and soil; all committed for our safety to its security and peace; preserved from annihilation only by the care, the work, and the love we give our fragile planet.

Adlai Stevenson (1900-1965)
Earth Day—The Beginning
(Bantam, 1970), p. 47

Modern man always tries to flee from himself. He can never be silent or alone, because that would mean to be alone with himself, and this is why the places of amusement and the cinemas are always filled with people. And when they find themselves

alone and are at a point where they might encounter God, they turn on the radio or the television set.

Ernesto Cardenal
To Live Is To Love
(Herder & Herder, 1972), p. 30

God of grace and God of glory,
On your people pour your pow'r;
Crown your ancient Church's story;
Bring its bud to glorious flow'r.
Grant us wisdom, grant us courage
For the facing of this hour,
For the facing of this hour.

Cure your children's warring madness;
Bend our pride to your control;
Shame our wanton, selfish gladness,
Rich in things and poor in soul.
Grant us wisdom, grant us courage,
Lest we miss your kingdom's goal.
Lest we miss your kingdom's goal.

Harry Emerson Fosdick (1878-1969)
Lutheran Book of Worship 415

8

Sin and Guilt

We have seen how our modern society is not living up to its polished image of itself. Far from solving every difficulty, we are drifting ever closer to personal, social, and ecological disaster. In spite of all our knowledge and power, something is wrong. Our century has been marked just as much by confusion, violence, and destruction as by technical progress. What is our problem?

1. Who is to blame?

In recent years some researchers have suggested that we are totally dependent on our heredity and environment. Assuming we are programmed by forces beyond our control, they argue that it makes no sense to talk about human freedom and responsibility. In spite of these extreme claims, almost everyone agrees that human beings have some responsibility for their actions. If our behavior is not what it should be, we are the ones who must ultimately be held responsible for it.

Judges and juries are constantly asked to decide the

guilt or innocence of individuals and corporations charged with crimes. Voters hold public officials responsible for what they do or don't do in office. Working people are given credit or blame for their job performance. Virtually the only people society excuses from responsibility are the mentally incompetent.

Our conscience also frequently reminds us that we are accountable for what we do. We experience feelings of guilt when we do not listen to it. As parents we may be troubled by the way we act toward our children. If we take something or someone that belongs to another, we may feel uneasy. If we drive recklessly and cause a death or serious injury, we may find it hard to live with ourselves. Such guilt feelings tell us that our conscience is alive and well.

Sometimes we have guilt feelings that have no basis in reality. These may come from anxiety, compulsive legalism, or depression. It is important to distinguish between genuine guilt feelings with a source in some actual error or failure and false guilt feelings that have no relationship to real failure. False guilt feelings may be a sign of psychological difficulty and may call for professional treatment.

Some people experience no guilt at all, regardless of what they do. They may have disregarded their conscience for so long that it has become deadened, or they may have a deeper problem. This is a very serious condition whenever it occurs, for the conscience is an indispensable guardian.

Some therapists actually believe we would be better

off if we could outgrow all our guilt feelings. Even they, however, recognize that guilt cannot just be ignored. When it is repressed it has a way of coming to the surface again in another form. It may return as an illness or neurosis. Guilt feelings may or may not be based on real failure, but they are real and must be recognized and dealt with.

2. What does the Bible say?

When the Bible talks about human responsibility, it uses the word *sin*. This word means many things to many people. For some, sin is limited to a misuse of sexuality. Dieters talk about eating as "sinful." Advertisers use the word to suggest that their products bring sensual pleasure. Is this what sin means? Is it a matter of losing our lingering inhibitions?

The Bible uses the word *sin* in two different ways. *Sin* refers both to particular *acts* of disobedience toward God and the human *condition* of being in a state of rebellion against God. In both cases the emphasis is on a broken relationship between God and human beings. We are *sinful,* and because of our desire to live without God we engage in *sins*.

According to the Bible, our basic human problem is wanting to be like God. Genesis 3 describes in story form our dissatisfaction with the creaturely role we have been given. We want to free ourselves from our dependence on God and on each other. We have gone beyond the bounds God had in mind for us. We

have declared our independence, and this is the root
of our problem.

The chapters from Genesis 3 to Genesis 11 depict
a natural progression from disobedience to God to
the consequences of this rebellion: pride, envy, murder. The story of Adam and Eve in the Garden of
Eden must be seen in the context of the chapters
that follow it. Sin is not just an individual act of disobedience; it begins with the desire to be like God
and results in disruption on every level of human
existence.

Created to live with God and respond to God's love,
human beings have separated themselves from that
love. We have declared ourselves to be the measure
of all things, refusing to pay attention to God's will.
The figure of Adam represents the entire human
race. In Adam we have all sinned (Rom. 5:12-13).
As we continue to disobey God's will, Adam's sin lives
on in us.

In the New Testament, Paul describes the life of
human beings under the power of sin as life "according to the flesh." By this phrase Paul does *not*
mean that life in the body is by nature evil. He also
speaks of fleshly life in a positive way (Gal. 2:20;
Phil. 1:22). Life "according to the flesh," however, is
a particular life-style of those who have separated
themselves from God and put their trust in things
that are earthly and transitory. Those who live according to the flesh base their reputations on what they
can show, on external assets such as property, or on

mental and spiritual assets such as education and religion. This attitude can influence everything we do.

The "works of the flesh" are not limited to "fornication, impurity, licentiousness"; they also include "enmity, strife, jealousy, anger, selfishness" (Gal. 5:19-21), the pride of religious people and the conceit of the sophisticated (Phil. 3:3-7), the spirit of worrisome concern that anxiously seeks to protect and secure life (1 Cor. 7:32; Matt. 6:25-26), and that boastful arrogance that constantly praises its own goodness, wisdom, strength, and importance (1 Cor. 1:19-31). Paul saw the consequences of living according to the flesh as slavery to the created world (1 Cor. 6:13-20; 7:23; 10:7).

The struggle that goes on inside a person between the desires of the world and the will of God is described in Paul's letter to the Romans:

I can will what is right, but I cannot do it. For I do not do the good I want, but the evil I do not want is what I do. Now if I do what I do not want, it is no longer I that do it, but sin which dwells within me.

So I find it to be a law that when I want to do right, evil lies close at hand. For I delight in the law of God, in my inmost self, but I see in my members another law at war with the law of my mind and making me captive to the law of sin which dwells in my members. Wretched man that I am! Who will deliver me from this body of death? (7:18-24)

According to Paul, sin is not just a particular evil

act, but a power that enslaves people. He describes the origin and consequences of this power in the imagery of Genesis 3: "Therefore as sin came into the world through one man and death through sin, and so death spread to all men because all men sinned . . ." (Rom. 5:12). For Paul, sin and death are inseparably linked to each other. Death is the result of rebellion against God (Gal. 6:8).

We can summarize the main points of Paul's understanding of sin as follows:

- Sin is a condition of trusting in something other than God.
- Sin is a power that takes control of persons.
- Sin permeates life and results in evil acts.
- The ultimate consequence of sin is death.

3. What is "original sin"?

The Bible's description of human nature, even in the simple story-language of Genesis, is far more accurate than optimistic portrayals of inevitable human progress. The effects of human sin have become painfully clear in our own century. Two world wars, the Holocaust, and atrocities such as My Lai have demonstrated how respectable, middle-class persons are capable of demonic brutality. Modern psychology recognizes the deep potential for aggression lying under our thin veneer of civilization.

Contemporary authors such as Arthur Miller, Kurt

Vonnegut, and Albert Camus have portrayed the evil
potential within us in a powerful way. Their novels
reveal people plagued by exploitive egoism and sinister forces, dangling like puppets on the strings of
their own greed. Scientific observation, historical experience, and literature all contradict the commonly
held opinion that human beings are basically pretty
good, that all we need to do is give them a little more
common sense.

In describing the depths of human evil and the
radical nature of our rebellion against God, Christian
faith uses the term "original sin." This teaching has
been much misunderstood. Basically, original sin
means four things:

Sin is universal

Sin is not simply something between God and individuals. Families, groups, and even whole peoples
can lose their relationship with God. From the day of
our birth we live in society, and society is the place
where egoism, indifference, and oppression occur. Sin
takes hold in the relationships between people.

We live in a tightly woven net of relationships. The
actions of individuals and groups link up with each
other to form sinful structures within society. Evil
then confronts us in both individual and corporate
forms. War, persecution, and oppression reveal sin in
its supra-personal form. No clear distinction can be
made between individual and corporate sin. Each
person is responsible, and yet each person shares in

the sin of society as a whole. It is not possible to excuse oneself, as Adam and Eve tried to do in Genesis 3.

Because sin also has corporate forms, not even "good" and "decent" people escape its grasp. No one is isolated from the larger human community; what we do affects others, and what others do affects us. There is nothing wrong with calling humble and faithful people "good." There is no need to cast them as sinister human beings. The doctrine of original sin insists, however, that no one can be morally isolated from what goes on in society.

Sin is unavoidable

The Christian faith has been criticized for teaching that everyone is a sinner from birth. How can someone, possibly be a sinner when he or she has not yet achieved a sense of conscious decision making?

Original sin does not mean that newborn babies commit evil acts. It means the roots of our human self-centeredness are present even at birth. A newborn baby is not very concerned about others. Its number one goal is having its own needs met. It uses the technique of crying to get the attention of its parents. As it grows, it learns other ways to get attention.

Sooner or later, a child has to learn to think about the needs of others. He or she must discover limits in order to function successfully in the world. This process is called socialization. Yet within every socialized and well-adjusted person is the same self-centered nature that was present at the beginning.

The doctrine of original sin points out that our greatest human need is to serve and worship God. Until we have been freed from our devotion to ourselves, this is impossible. Neither a child nor an adult naturally loves God above all else. This comes only from outside, as a gift. Only God can work in us so we genuinely love him and other people.

Sin brings guilt

The Bible insists that no matter how noble or strong a person may be, he or she is not whole apart from a relationship with God. It is not enough to say, "I live a good life. I don't hurt anyone." This attitude reflects the pride that is at the heart of our sinful condition. Sin is fundamentally not a matter of what we *do* but in whom we *trust*. If we trust in ourselves more than we trust in God, we are guilty of sin, and our actions will reflect our orientation.

Independence from God seems attractive, but it results in pride, judging of others, and perhaps despair if we should lose confidence in ourselves. The Bible declares that no one has an excuse—everyone is guilty of living their lives apart from God (Rom. 3:23).

We human beings are not content to live as God's creatures, trusting in him. We desire the kind of freedom and independence God alone has. Rebelling from our creaturely role, we find an independence that is not freedom at all, but slavery to ourselves. In the

process we lose God, violate our neighbors, and lay waste to creation. Our no to God wells up from deep within us, confirmed by each destructive thing we do.

Sin produces sins

Sin is usually thought of in terms of *sins*, individual acts that are wrong. This is only natural, for our sinful actions are the symptoms of our sickness—our rebellion. Different societies have different ways to judge the seriousness of sins. Usually an evil deed is considered worse than a bad word, a deliberate act of violence is seen as more serious than an accident. These distinctions are necessary in the moral and legal areas of life, but they become misleading when applied to our relationship with God. It is all too easy to start the familiar process of self-justification by comparing our actions with those of others.

Jesus saw the accounting of good and evil actions as an attempt to avoid true understanding of ourselves and repentance. He showed how our evil acts originate in our heart. Sin, he said, could not be limited to actions, but is already present in evil thoughts (Matt. 5:21-48). Jesus was not denying distinctions in morality; he was emphasizing that in the eyes of God no one can insist on his or her own righteousness (Luke 18:9-14).

During the Middle Ages the church identified "seven deadly sins": sloth, pride, greed, lust, envy, gluttony, and wrath. Luther came to the conclusion that every sin is "deadly," because every sin expresses our separation from God. Good works cannot cover up our problem, either. We are in no position to bargain with God on the basis of what we do or don't do. God owes us nothing. We owe God everything. When we refuse to worship and serve him above all else, we sin. Luther *did* distinguish between sin that is under control and sin that controls us. Christians are both sinners and saints at the same time. We always stand in need of God's forgiveness.

Summary

● If our behavior is not what it should be, we are the ones who must ultimately be held responsible for it.

● Guilt feelings are real and must be recognized and dealt with.

● When the Bible talks about human responsibility, it uses the word *sin*.

● *Sin* refers both to particular *acts* of disobedience toward God and the human *condition* of being in a state of rebellion against God.

● The Bible's description of human nature, even in the simple story-language of Genesis, is far more accurate than optimistic portrayals of inevitable human progress.

● The doctrine of "original sin" means sin is *universal, unavoidable, brings guilt,* and *produces sins*.

For reflection

There is no distinction; since all have sinned and
fall short of the glory of God. . . .

Rom. 3:22-23

Today your mercy calls us
To wash away our sin.
However great our trespass,
Whatever we have been,
However long from mercy
Our hearts have turned away,
Your precious blood can wash us,
And make us clean today.

Oswald Allen (1816-1878)
Lutheran Book of Worship 304

Many modern psychologists tell us always to dis-
trust this vague feeling of guilt, as something purely
pathological. And if they had stopped at that, I might
believe them. But when they go on, as some do, to
apply the same treatment to all guilt feelings whatever, to suggest that one's feeling about a particular
unkind act or a particular insincerity is also and
equally untrustworthy—I can't help thinking they are
talking nonsense. One sees this the moment one looks
at other people. I have talked to some who felt
guilt when they jolly well ought to have felt it; they

have behaved like brutes and know it. I've also met
others who felt guilty and weren't guilty by any
standard I can apply. And thirdly, I've met people
who were guilty and didn't seem to feel guilt.

C. S. Lewis (1898-1963)
Letters to Malcolm
(Harcourt, Brace & World, 1963), pp. 32-33

Sin lies in the will, not in the intellect; and this
corruption of the will goes well beyond the consciousness of the individual . . . otherwise the question of
how sin began must arise with respect to each individual.

Søren Kierkegaard (1813-1855)
Sickness unto Death
(Princeton, 1941), p. 155

We do not like words such as "sin" and "punishment." They seem to us old-fashioned, barbaric, and
invalid in the light of modern psychology. But whenever I have met exiles of high moral standards and
insight, I have discovered that they feel responsible
for what has happened within their own countries.
And very often I have met citizens of democratic
countries, citizens of this country, who have expressed
a feeling of guilt for the situation of the world today.

They were right, and the exiles were right; they are responsible, as are you and I. Whether or not we call it sin, whether or not we call it punishment, we are beaten by the consequences of our own failures. That is the order of history.

Paul Tillich (1886-1965)
The Shaking of the Foundations
(Scribner's, 1948), p. 19

I have failed again, O Lord.
Despite my firm resolutions
and determined efforts,
I have flopped—fallen on my face.
And I come limping back to you.

Leslie F. Brandt
Book of Christian Prayer
(Augsburg, 1980), p. 91, adapted

9

Evil and Deliverance

Most of us do not want to face the truth about ourselves. We would rather compare ourselves with others than confess our common rebellion against God. It is easier to believe we are open and accepting persons than admit to our stubborn pride. We prefer to count up the good things we have done than imagine that, under the right circumstances, we are capable of inhuman cruelty.

Yet if we are sensitive to the voice of our conscience and the realities of the world we have fashioned, we cannot completely ignore the truth. We seem to be trapped within our self-centered life-styles—bound to a power that prevents us from truly loving God and honestly caring for others. What is this force that binds us to ourselves, and how can we be freed from it?

1. What binds us?

Evil is more than the sum total of our individual rebellions against God. We experience evil as a power that binds us to our sin and defies all our efforts to

free ourselves. Evil has a depth and a presence far
stronger than we are.

When the Bible talks about the radical nature of
evil, it refers to "the devil." In picture language it uses
the figure of the devil to represent the fact that evil
goes far beyond every human possibility. So often that
which is evil has a more powerful attraction for us
than that which is good. Things that have taken years
to build can be destroyed in seconds. Restoration can
never be accomplished so easily. Neither delusion nor
aggression are adequate explanations for something
like Auschwitz. Nothing but a demonic personification
of evil can give sufficient expression to its horror.

The evil in this world does not consist of a few
regrettable flaws that are easily fixed. The Nazi plan
for a "final solution" to the Jewish question shows
that evil can be systematic and methodical. A news-
paper once posed the question, "Do you believe there
is a hell in which the devil rules?" The bishop of
Stockholm responded, "I don't believe it—I see it!" His
words reflect what the church means when it speaks
of the devil. There is a radical and destructive evil
power in the world that opposes God and his creation
and enslaves human beings.

The devil is not the only power besides God and
human beings mentioned in the Bible. The Bible also
talks about "angels." Christians throughout the ages
have sensed God's sheltering presence around them.
One of the ways they have spoken of this presence
is with the imagery of angels.

In our time, belief in good forces such as guardian angels seems to have faded even more than belief in the demonic. The church's most significant festival commemorating angels, the festival of St. Michael and All Angels (celebrated on September 29), has been all but forgotten. Yet according to the Bible, God is not solitary and unapproachable. He is a ruling King on a throne, surrounded by angelic beings, seraphim and cherubim (Isa. 6:1-4; Rev. 4:1-8). Angelic choirs gathered around the throne constantly sing God's praise (Ps. 148:2).

Luther insisted on keeping the festival of St. Michael, the archangel, in order to give due respect to the biblical teaching about angels. He saw belief in angels primarily as a help in overcoming temptation. Angels are not to be worshiped; they have no power to forgive anyone's sins. They are God's messengers and servants. In Luther's St. Michael's Day sermons, Christ remains central, the sovereign helper in our struggle with the forces of evil.

2. How are we delivered?

Where do we find solid ground to stand on in overcoming evil in ourselves and in our world? Obviously we do not find it in ourselves. According to the Bible, this ground is found only in the love of God manifested in Jesus Christ. Christian churches everywhere agree with this witness. Nevertheless, there are different understandings of humanity and different in-

terpretations of the work of Christ. Some of the different accents can be summarized as follows:

● Because of original sin, we are completely incapable of appeasing God's anger. God himself, represented in Christ, achieves satisfaction for human sin.

● Our relationship to God may be disrupted, but Christ is our God-given aid. In him, God has provided an example for us to follow.

● We live in between good and evil. Both light and darkness are in us. We can be saved by accepting Jesus Christ and giving our lives to him.

● We are totally bound to ourselves in matters related to our salvation. Yet as participants in Jesus' resurrection through Baptism, we are also completely free to love God. We are saints and sinners at the same time.

In each of these expressions of Christ's work, God is seen as encountering us on a level other than the one we imagine ourselves to be on. God does not wait until we have changed or bettered ourselves. He does not judge us by the past from which we have come, but by the future toward which we are headed.

God judges us:

● not by what we are, but by what we will be.
● not by what we do for him, but by what he does for us.

- not by what we offer him, but by what he offers us.
- not by our accomplishments, but by his love.

Even as we confess our sin, God has already begun his work of renewal in us. God's love is always stronger than our sin. How do we know? Jesus Christ has told us about the power of this love. He embodied it, revealed it, and demonstrated it. It was the occasion for such opposition by people that he eventually died for it. In Christ, God himself loved us to the point of death. As a result, our deepest conflict has been resolved. God has countered our mistrust with his trust, our hatred with his love, our self-assertion with his self-surrender.

Neither the devil nor the angels are independent powers, battling each other over the fate of human beings. God's judgment concerning us has already been made in Christ, who has won the victory over sin, death, and the devil. God has decided in our favor and embraced us with his love, even if we do not realize it.

Summary

- Evil has a depth and a presence that is far stronger than we are.
- There is a radical and destructive evil power in the world that opposes God and his creation and enslaves human beings.

● According to the Bible, God is not solitary and unapproachable. He is a ruling King on a throne, surrounded by angelic beings.

● God does not judge us by the past from which we have come, but by the future toward which we are headed.

● God has countered our mistrust with his trust, our hatred with his love, our self-assertion with his self-surrender.

● God's judgment concerning us has already been made in Christ, who has won the victory over sin, death, and the devil.

For reflection

He (the devil) was a murderer from the beginning, and has nothing to do with the truth, because there is no truth in him. When he lies, he speaks according to his own nature, for he is a liar and the father of lies.

John 8:44

Though hordes of devils fill the land
All threat'ning to devour us,
We tremble not, unmoved we stand;
They cannot overpower us.
This world's prince may rage,
In fierce war engage.
He is doomed to fail;

God's judgment must prevail!
One little word subdues him.

Martin Luther (1483-1546)
Lutheran Book of Worship 228

If angels no longer came to people, this world would
go to pieces. As long as God sustains the earth he
will send his angels.

Angels are older than any and all religion. Indeed,
they still come even to people who do not want to
hear anything about religion.

Claus Westermann
God's Angels Need No Wings
(Fortress, 1979), p. 11

There are times in history when evil can be explained as deserved punishment, others when no such
explanation is possible—when divine Power is, "as it
were," suspended, and God Himself suffers in exile.
Such openness is necessary if history is to be serious.

Emil Fackenheim
Quest for Past and Future
(Beacon, 1968), p. 17

Absolute evil imposes itself upon creation in the
form that we all recognize, namely, sin and death. It

appears in the illegitimate dominion, incomprehensible and inexplicable, of the one whom the Scriptures call the Devil. The creature is defenseless in the face of this threat. God is superior to it, but not the creature. Once given entrance, the Devil performs endless ravages against which we have no other protection than God's. Wherever God is absent, wherever he is not the master, it is the other one who dominates. There is no alternative.

Karl Barth (1886-1968)
Prayer
(Westminster, 1952), p. 73

Lord, how do I deal with evil?
How do I find my way through all the suffering
in the world and not give up?
What do I do in all the wickedness?
What do I do in those tempting times,
when it's hard to be in
and hard to stay out?
Be with me in those times.
I will deal with evil while living in it.
I know there is evil, Lord, and I know there is good.
Both are here,
and I am deciding about them, Jesus.

Herbert F. Brokering
Surprise Me, Jesus
(Augsburg, 1973), p. 58

Part Four

Who Is Jesus?

We follow a God who took upon himself our human condition, One who had a history like ours, who lived our experiences, who made choices, who devoted himself to a cause for which he suffered, who had successes, joys, and failures, for which he gave his life. . . .

It is only through Jesus of Nazareth that we can know God, his words, his deeds, his ideals, his demands. It is in Jesus that the true God reveals himself: all-powerful but at the same time poor and suffering for love; absolute, but also someone with his own human history, someone close to every person.

Segundo Galilea
Following Jesus
(Orbis, 1981), pp. 12-13

10

Scripture and History

Our chronological distance from the historical Jesus is very great. We know of him only through a few documents that present different viewpoints. In the oldest surviving non-Christian reports, Jesus is mentioned only incidentally and seems to be relatively unimportant. On the other hand, the earliest Christian sources revolve around him. For them Jesus is the most significant person in history. These Christian writings are much more than historical reports. Many people have questioned their reliability as objective history, yet they are virtually the only sources we have about Jesus' life and message. We cannot avoid turning to them if we want to find out who this person was and is.

1. The New Testament as a historical source

The most important and absolutely indispensable source of information about Jesus is the New Testament. The entire collection, with all of its individual "books," bears witness to him. The four gospels provide the most vivid and detailed accounts about Jesus.

The first three (Matthew, Mark, and Luke), called the *synoptic* gospels because they see Jesus in a similar way, are closely related. The gospel of John has its own special character. Compared with the four gospels, the other books of the New Testament contain noticeably fewer references to Jesus' life and mission, words and actions. Some of the letters ascribed to the apostle Paul, however, are the oldest known Christian documents, having been written between 50 and 65 A.D. Their chronological closeness to the life of Jesus is even more significant because they contain early Christian hymns and statements of faith (for example, Phil. 2:6-11; 1 Cor. 15:3-7). The statements of faith usually focus on the declaration, "Jesus died and was raised again." Paul also summarized the life of Jesus in the words, "born of woman, born under the law" (Gal. 4:4). Paul's quotation of Jesus' words shows that he was acquainted with his sayings.

The Gospels are, first and foremost, witnesses to the early Christians' faith in Jesus. They present the life of Jesus in the light of his death and resurrection, the two focal points of the early confessions of faith. The Gospels preserve many stories that were told and retold in the earliest Christian communities. In the beginning these were passed on orally. As the number of living eyewitnesses to Jesus' life and ministry began to diminish, the oral traditions were collected and written down. In this way Christian communities prevented Jesus' message from being distorted.

In recent times several attempts have been made to discredit Jesus as a historical person and portray him as the creation of pious fantasy. The scarcity of early non-Christian reports about Jesus was viewed as support for this theory. Today, even though such theories are heard occasionally, few historians take them seriously. There is little doubt that Jesus was a person of this world and a participant in its history.

It is true that the earliest non-Christian reports date from the end of the first century, but these show that even opponents of Christianity did not doubt Jesus' existence. In addition, while the Gospels are not historical biographies, they show every sign of being firmly anchored in historical events.

Even if we limit ourselves to those facts about Jesus that are beyond all reasonable doubt, we can safely say the following things about him:

- He was a Jew.
- His mother's name was Mary.
- He grew up in Nazareth in Galilee.
- He was a carpenter by trade.
- He was baptized by John the Baptist.
- His ministry took place first in Galilee and then in Judea.
- He was condemned to death by the Roman procurator Pontius Pilate during the time of a Passover festival in Jerusalem.
- He was executed on a cross.

All these facts are important, and yet without knowing more about what Jesus said and did, they would probably be of little interest to us.

If we want to know who Jesus was and is, we must know more than the bare historical facts. We must come to grips with who the Christian community *believed him to be*. This is what the four gospels, in their various ways, set out to tell us. The stories they tell about Jesus are grounded in history, but that is not the primary reason the Gospels tell them. The gospel writers were not writing complete biographies, but explaining *who Jesus was and is*. It is impossible to completely separate history from faith in the Gospels. They always bind the two closely together.

We know something about the linkage of faith and history from our own lives:

● Only those things that touch us personally really influence us. Things must affect us in some meaningful way in order to hit home.

● In reports about daily events—even those we have witnessed ourselves—it is impossible to separate what actually happened from personal impressions of what happened. For example, witnesses to traffic accidents often give conflicting accounts of the same event.

● We can fully describe people only when we have some personal contact with them. A list of bare facts never does justice to them. We must also include our personal impressions.

ΚΑΙΕΙΠΕΝΠΡΟСΑΥ
ΤΟΥСΠΡΑΓΜΑΤΕΥ
СΘΑΙΕΝΩΕΡΧΟΜΑΙ
ΟΙΔΕΠΟΛΕΙΤΑΙΑΥΤ
ΕΜΙСΟΥΝΑΥΤΟΝΚ
ΑΠΕСΤΙΛΑΝΠΡΕС
ΒΕΙΑΝΟΠΙСΩΑΥΤΟ
ΛΕΓΟΝΤΕСΟΥΘΕΛ
ΤΟΥΤΟΝΒΑСΙΛΕΥСΑΙ
ΕΦΗΜΑСΚΑΙΕΓΕΝΕ
ΤΟΕΝΤΩΕΠΑΝΕΛ
ΑΥΤΟΝΛΑΒΟΝΤΑΤΗ
ΒΑСΙΛΕΙΑΝΚΑΙΕΙΠ
ΦΩΝΗΘΗΝΑΙΑΥΤ
ΤΟΥСΔΟΥΛΟΥСΤΟΥ
ΤΟΥСΟΙСΔΕΔΩΚΕΙ
ΤΟΑΡΓΥΡΙΟΝΙΝΑΓΝ
ΤΙΔΙΕΠΡΑΓΜΑΤΕΥСΑ
ΤΟ ΠΑΡΕΓΕΝΕΤΟ
ΔΕΟΠΡΩΤΟСΛΕΓΩ
ΚΕΗΜΝΑСΟΥΔΕΚΑ
ΠΡΟСΕΙΡΓΑСΑΜΝΑС
ΚΑΙΕΙΠΕΝΑΥΤΩ
ΔΟΥΛΕΑΓΑΘΕΟΤΙ
ΕΝΕΛΑΧΙСΤΩΠΙС
ΕΓΕΝΟΥΙСΘΙΕΞΟΥ
ΑΝΕΧΩΝΕΠΑΝΩ
ΔΕΚΑΠΟΛΕΩΝ
ΚΑΙΗΛΘΕΝΟΔΕΥΤ
ΡΟСΛΕΓΩΝΗΜΝΑ
СΟΥΚΕΕΠΟΙΗСΕΝ
ΠΕΝΤΕΜΝΑС·
ΕΙΠΕΝΔΕΚΑΙΤΟΥ
ΤΩΚΑΙСΥΕΠΑΝΩ
ΓΕΙΝΟΥΠΕΝΤΕΠΟ
ΛΕΩΝ
ΚΑΙΟΕΤΕΡΟСΗΛΘΕΝ
ΛΕΓΩΝΚΕΙΔΟΥΗ
ΜΝΑСΟΥΗΝΕΙΧΟ
ΑΠΟΚΕΙΜΕΝΗΝ
СΟΥΔΑΡΙΩΕΦΟ
ΡΟΥΜΗΝΓΑΡСΕΟΤΙ
ΑΝΘΡΩΠΟСΑΥСΤΗ
ΡΟСΕΙΑΙΡΙСΟΟΥΚ
ΕΘΗΚΑСΚΑΙΘΕΡΙ
ΖΕΙСΟΟΥΚΕСΠΙΡΑ
ΛΕΓΕΙΑΥΤΩΕΚΤΟΥ

СΤΟΜΑΤΟССΟΥΚΡΙ
ΝΩСΕΠΟΝΗΡΕΔΟ
ΛΕΗΔΙСΟΤΙΕΓΩΑΝ
ΘΡΩΠΟСΑΥСΤΗ
ΕΙΜΙΑΙΡΩΝΟΟΥΚ
ΕΘΗΚΑΚΑΙΘΕΡΙΖΩ
ΟΟΥΚΕСΠΙΡΑΚΑΙ
ΔΙΑΤΙΟΥΚΕΔΩΚΑ
ΜΟΥΤΟΑΡΓΥΡΙΟΝ
ΕΠΙΤΡΑΠΕΖΑΝΚΑ
ΓΩΕΛΘΩΝСΥΝΤΟ
ΤΟΚΩΑΝΑΥΤΟΕ
ΠΡΑΞΑΚΑΙΤΟΙСΠΑ
ΡΕСΤΩСΙΝΕΙΠΕΝ
ΑΡΑΤΕΑΠΑΥΤΟΥΤΗΝ
ΜΝΑΝΚΑΙΔΟΤΕΤ
ΤΑСΔΕΚΑΜΝΑСΕΧΟ
ΤΙΚΑΙΕΙΠΑΝΑΥΤ
ΚΕΕΧΕΙΔΕΚΑΜΝΑ
ΛΕΓΩΟΤΙΠΑΝΤΙΤ
ΕΧΟΝΤΙΔΟΘΗСΕ
ΤΑΙΑΠΟΔΕΤΟΥΜΗ
ΕΧΟΝΤΟСΚΑΙΟΕ
ΧΕΙΑΡΘΗСΕΤΑΙΑΠΑΥΤΟΥ
ΠΛΗΝΤΟΥСΕΧΘΡ
ΜΟΥΤΟΥΤΟΥСΤΟ
ΜΗΘΕΛΗСΑΝΤΑС
ΜΕΒΑСΙΛΕΥСΑΙΕ
ΠΑΥΤΟΥСΑΓΑΓΕΤ
ΩΔΕΚΑΙΚΑΤΑСΦΑ
ΞΕΤΕΑΥΤΟΥСΕΜ
ΠΡΟСΘΕΝΜΟΥ
ΚΑΙΕΙΠΩΝΤΑΥΤΑ
ΠΟΡΕΥΕΤΟΕΜΠΡ
СΘΕΝΑΝΑΒΑΙΝΩ
ΕΙСΙΕΡΟСΟΛΥΜΑ
ΚΑΙΕΓΕΝΕΤΟΩСΗΓ
ΓΙСΕΝΕΙСΒΗΘΦΑ
ΓΗΚΑΙΒΗΘΑΝΙΑ
ΠΡΟСΤΟΟΡΟСΤΟ
ΚΑΛΟΥΜΕΝΟΝ
ΩΝ
ΑΠΕСΤΙΛΕΝΔΥΟ
ΤΩΝΜΑΘΗΤΩΝ
ΛΕΓΩΝΥΠΑΓΕΤΕ
ΤΗΝΚΑΤΕΝΑΝΤΙ
ΚΩΜΗΝΕΝΗ
ΠΟΡΕΥΟΜΕΝΟΙΥ

Personal accounts communicate more, not less, than factual descriptions. This is particularly true for anyone who has met Jesus, who has been captivated by his story and feels compelled to talk about it. The New Testament needs to be read in this light.

2. The Bible as Scripture

Unlike some religions, Judaism and Christianity are based on particular historical events. The central event in Israel's history was the exodus from Egypt. The Christian community found its focus in the death and resurrection of Jesus. For this reason, written accounts of God's actions in history have been extremely important to Jews and Christians. They transmit the stories of what God has said and done in human history from one generation to another.

The first Christian communities looked to the Scriptures of Israel for keys to understanding Jesus. At that time the Jewish Scriptures included the Law (the first five books of the Bible), the Prophets, and the Writings (such as Psalms, Proverbs, and the later historical books). These books, all of which are included in the Old Testament, were interpreted in the light of what Jesus had said and done, and Jesus was interpreted in the light of these books, understood as Scripture.

About the middle of the second century A.D. the church began to develop lists of specifically Christian writings that were to be considered authoritative.

Books were included in the "canon"—the definitive list—if they were "apostolic" (old and apparently written by an apostle) and agreed with the content of the unquestionably genuine apostolic writings.

The use of the New Testament books within the Christian church for preaching and teaching throughout the centuries has confirmed the fact that God speaks to people through them. Even though there was no formal decree about the list of books in the canon until the time of the Reformation, the whole Christian church agrees that the 27 books of the New Testament are inspired by God. They are called the "Word of God," together with the Old Testament, because through them God's word comes to us.

The Old Testament provides a context for understanding Jesus. The New Testament preserves for us the original teachings of the apostles. Bound together by a common link of faith in the God of Israel, the books of the Bible are one of the treasures of the church. They provide every generation with knowledge of Jesus and the context necesssary to understand him.

Christians of earlier times thought the Bible had only one point of view. Recent studies have shown that there is great diversity among the books of the Bible. Different biblical writers had different perspectives and emphases. There are even some details that contradict each other. These discoveries have created feelings of uncertainty among some Christians about the authority of the Bible. Yet the authority of the

Bible does not depend on the total consistency of every detail, but on the God whose word and will are revealed through it. What unites all the books of the New Testament is the Lord Jesus Christ to whom each one bears witness.

3. Interpreting the Bible

The world in which the Bible was written was very different from ours, and it is sometimes hard to understand passages from this ancient collection of books. We need to translate and interpret the Bible's language and thought-forms if we are to make sense of its message.

When we want to understand a biblical text, we should begin by asking what it originally meant. Unless we try to determine the original meaning, it is all too easy for us to read into a text something that isn't there. We can look at the original Hebrew and Greek words and their meaning, the construction of the sentences, and the overall organization of the particular segment. At the very least we must look at the context of the passage and the historical situation and environment of the writer.

Once we have done our best to understand what a biblical text *meant,* we are ready to ask what it *means.* This second task is by far the more difficult of the two. There are many different methods of biblical interpretation. Each method, however, tries to explain the connection between what God did for his people in the past and what God is doing for people today.

Martin Luther emphasized that the entire Bible must be understood in the light of what God has done in Jesus Christ. The very word *gospel* ("good news") points to the person of Christ as the heart of the Christian faith. He is the center of what God has done for us, and therefore he is the center of the Bible, the one to whom everything else must be related.

Summary

• The Gospels are, first and foremost, witnesses to the early Christians' faith in Jesus.

• Personal accounts communicate more, not less, than factual descriptions.

• Unlike some world religions, Judaism and Christianity are based on particular historical events.

• The Bible provides every generation with knowledge of Jesus and the context necessary to understand him.

• What unites the books of the New Testament is the Lord Jesus Christ to whom each bears witness.

• We need to translate and interpret the Bible's language and thought-forms if we are to make sense of its message today.

For reflection

All scripture is inspired by God and profitable for

teaching, for reproof, for correction, and for training in righteousness. . . .

2 Tim. 3:16

One should thus realize that there is only one gospel, but that it is described by many apostles. Every single epistle of Paul and of Peter, as well as the Acts of the Apostles by Luke, is a gospel, even though they do not record all the works and words of Christ, but one is shorter and includes less than another. There is not one of the four major gospels anyway that includes all the words and works of Christ; nor is this necessary. Gospel is and should be nothing else than a discourse or story about Christ, just as happens among men when one writes a book about a king or a prince, telling what he did, said, and suffered in his day. Such a story can be told in various ways; one spins it out, and the other is brief.

Martin Luther (1483-1546)
Luther's Works, vol. 35
(Fortress, 1960), p. 117

When we study history and amuse ourselves with stories, we are always wanting to know: How did it all happen? How is it that one event follows another? What are the natural causes of things? *Why* did the people speak such words and live such lives? It is just at the most decisive points of its history that the Bible gives no answer to our Why. . . . But we may not deny nor prevent our being led by Bible "history" far out beyond what is elsewhere called history—into a new world, into the world of God.

Karl Barth (1886-1968)
The Word of God and the Word of Man
(Harper & Bros., 1957), pp. 35, 37

Biblical stories are not props for pious schemes already thought beforehand. God's Word is a power that pries open reality and questions the philosophies that seek to interpret it. Reality is asked a new question by God's Word.

Frederick Herzog
Liberation Theology
(Seabury, 1972), p. 18

The Bible is not an end but a beginning; a precedent, not a story—the perennial motion of the spirit. It is a book that cannot die, that is incapable of becoming stale or obsolete. Oblivion shuns its pages. Its power is not subsiding. In fact, it is still at the very beginning of its career, the full meaning of its content having hardly touched the threshold of our minds; like an ocean at the bottom of which countless pearls lie; waiting to be discovered, its spirit is still to be unfolded. . . . What would be missing in the world, what would be the condition and faith of man, had the Bible not been preserved?

Abraham Joshua Heschel (1907-1972)
Israel: An Echo of Eternity
(Farrar, Straus & Giroux, 1967), pp. 46-47

God's Word is our great heritage
And shall be ours forever;
To spread its light from age to age
Shall be our chief endeavor.
Through life it guides our way;
In death it is our stay.
Lord, grant while time shall last
Your Church may hold it fast
Throughout all generations.

Nikolai F. S. Grundtvig (1783-1872)
Lutheran Book of Worship 239

11

Jesus in the Gospels

We have seen that the Gospels were not written as biographies in the modern sense. They tell the story of Jesus, but they are less concerned with a listing of facts about him than with who he was and what he said and did. Everything the Gospels tell us about Jesus communicates something about his person and what he meant to those who believed in him.

What then do the Gospels say about Jesus? How do they present him? What sort of a picture do they paint of this man from Nazareth?

1. Jesus' mission and teachings

Jesus grew up in Nazareth as the oldest son of a family that traced its ancestry from David. When John the Baptist appeared at the Jordan River, Jesus allowed himself to be baptized by him. At this point his public ministry began. Like the Old Testament prophets and John himself, Jesus considered himself to have been sent by God to the whole people of Israel.

The ministry of Jesus took place in a period of Is-

rael's history that was full of burning expectations; the
people chafed under Roman rule and looked for a
messenger from God to save them from their troubles.
Jesus announced that "the time is fulfilled, and the
kingdom of God is at hand" (Mark 1:15). The God
of Israel would reveal himself to human beings in
grace and judgment. The prophets long before had
promised that God's kingdom would come. But what
the prophets saw in the distant future was for Jesus
already breaking into the present. It was time to "repent, and believe in the gospel" (Mark 1:15).

Jesus' parables show that his understanding of
God's kingdom conflicted with the standard notions
held by his contemporaries. For example, he saw
children as model recipients of the kingdom (Mark
10:14). He compared the kingdom to "a grain of mus-
tard seed, which, when sown upon the ground, is the
smallest of all the seeds on earth; yet when it is sown
it grows up and becomes the greatest of all shrubs"
(Mark 4:30-32), and to leaven which, despite its
small amount, leavens the entire dough (Matt. 13:33).
The kingdom of God is like the earth, he said, which
of itself brings forth fruit without our doing anything
(Mark 4:26-29). In telling such parables, Jesus made
it clear that God's kingdom is very different from our
human notions of what a kingdom is.

Jesus acted much like a Jewish rabbi or teacher.
He taught in the synagogues and debated his opponents. People asked him questions about the meaning and application of the commandments. He was

acknowledged as an authority in the interpretation of Scripture. He broke through complicated and legalistic interpretations of the commandments to the original will of God: the command to love God with our whole heart and our neighbors as ourselves. We are not to barricade ourselves behind "correct" fulfillment of human regulations. Instead, we are to direct our attention toward those around us. God's will is that people be freed, not burdened: "the sabbath was made for man, not man for the sabbath" (Mark 2:27).

In the parable of the good Samaritan (Luke 10:25-37), the people whose occupations called on them to express God's love—a priest and a levite—passed their neighbor by. By comparison, a Samaritan, whose religious faith was considered questionable, spontaneously demonstrated love to his neighbor. In telling this story Jesus showed that to love God without loving our neighbors is absurd. Jesus also made this point through his own actions. He immersed himself in the task of meeting the needs of people, yet he also spent much time alone in prayer.

Jesus' preaching was given credibility by the consistency between his words and his actions. He showed love, compassion, faithfulness, peaceableness, dedication, self-renunciation, and forgiveness in his dealings with children, women, the ill, and all who were in need. Samaritans, tax collectors, and the poor—the very people rejected or avoided by others—were accepted by Jesus. He ate with known sinners who were condemned by others. When people said, "This man receives sinners and eats with them" (Luke 15:2), he responded with the parable of the lost son (Luke 15:11-32). He insisted he was obeying God's will: "I came not to call the righteous, but sinners" (Mark 2:17).

The hardness of some of Jesus' words (Matt. 18:6), the severity of the demands he laid on those who wanted to follow him (Luke 9:57-62), and his clashes with those who opposed him (Matthew 23) appear to conflict with the ideals of mercy and love. Yet Jesus understood himself to be faithful to the God who is not only a loving Father but also a righteous Judge, exposing the pride and self-centeredness of human beings.

Jesus performed certain unique deeds that heightened the impression of his power. These "miracles" are referred to in the Gospels as "signs and wonders." They were not performed for their own sake, but to indicate that God is the victor over illness and misfortune, over death and the evil one. Jesus demonstrated by means of them that God the Creator wanted to restore his creation and his creatures to wholeness.

Jesus' signs, like his words, proclaimed the imminent approach of God's kingdom: "If it is by the finger of God that I cast out demons, then the kingdom of God has come upon you" (Luke 11:20). Jesus consistently refused to prove himself through signs: "An evil and adulterous generation seeks for a sign" (Matt. 16:4). Signs are always ambiguous. Only those who are open to God's activity in their lives recognize signs

JESUS IN THE GOSPELS 177

for what they are. Others will find explanations for
them. The true miracle Jesus spoke about was God's
revelation of himself. All other signs were just hints
of its nearness.

In the Judaism of Jesus' day it was common for respected rabbis to gather disciples (students) to pass
on their insights. Jesus also gathered disciples around
himself, but with some differences from the usual
custom:

● Usually students chose their teacher. Jesus re-
versed this practice by choosing his own disciples.

● The goal of a disciple was eventually to leave his
teacher and establish his own circle of disciples. Jesus' disciples remained with him until the end. Even
after Jesus' death, their attention remained focused
on him.

Jesus gave prayer a central place in the life of faith.
He provided his disciples with a personal example of
prayerful living and taught them how to pray (Matt.
6:9-13; Luke 11:2-4):

Our Father in heaven,
hallowed be your name,
your kingdom come,
your will be done,
on earth as in heaven.
Give us today our daily bread.
Forgive us our sins
as we forgive those

who sin against us.
Save us from the time of trial
and deliver us from evil (ICET).

The disciples were urged to follow Jesus' example in maintaining a close relationship to God through prayer. "Ask, and it will be given you; seek, and you will find; knock, and it will be opened to you" (Luke 11:9).

2. The crucified Messiah

When Jesus declared, "the kingdom of God is at hand" (Mark 1:15), he meant that in some sense the kingdom was breaking into the world through his own ministry. Through his words, his actions, and his companionship with society's outcasts, he was already anticipating the kingdom's presence. He proclaimed himself to be the one through whom God's kingdom was coming. He identified himself with the long-expected Messiah—the anointed king—that God would send to free his people.

The claims Jesus made offended people. The residents of his home town of Nazareth were outraged that a simple carpenter, known to everyone, should claim such authority. They said, " 'Where did this man get all this? What is the wisdom given to him? What mighty works are wrought by his hands! Is not this the carpenter, the son of Mary and brother of James and Joses and Judas and Simon, and are not his

sisters here with us?" And they took offense at him"
(Mark 6:2-3).

Jesus' public ministry lasted only two or three years.
Opposition to him gradually began to build. He had
attracted a significant following, and the religious and
political authorities considered him a threat. His disciples were aware of the dangers and urged him not
to travel to Jerusalem. The Gospels say he disregarded their advice and "set his face to go to Jerusalem" (Luke 9:51).

Jesus arrived in Jerusalem and began to preach and
teach shortly before the festival of Passover. Jesus
celebrated the Passover meal with his disciples in an
upper room. Later that night he was betrayed and
arrested.

The circumstances of Jesus' trial are not completely
clear, but he seems to have been questioned by both
Jewish and Roman authorities. The Romans did not
allow the Jews to execute anyone, so it was definitely
Pontius Pilate who sentenced him to death. The date
of his crucifixion is difficult to determine, but the best
estimates point to the year 30 A.D. on a day in the
Jewish calendar that would have been April 7. The
fact that it was a Friday is much more certain.

The earliest gospel to be written—Mark—states that
Jesus' last words from the cross were, "My God, my
God, why hast thou forsaken me?" (Mark 15:34)
These words were not just a cry of despair, but also a
prayer to God (Ps. 22:1). Luke reports Jesus to have
said, "Father, into thy hands I commit my spirit!"

(23:46) According to John, he died shortly after saying, "It is finished" (19:30). In these different ways the gospel writers offer glimpses of the meaning and significance of the death of Jesus of Nazareth.

3. The resurrected Lord

The entire New Testament is filled with the certainty that Jesus did not remain dead, but rose from the grave. He was raised by God to new life and is now the Lord of all.

A variety of witnesses express this certainty. One of the oldest Easter accounts is found not in the Gospels, but in the apostle Paul's first letter to the Corinthians (15:3-7). There he repeats a confession of faith he had received. In addition, Paul mentions the names of eyewitnesses who were still living at the time his letter was written. Paul does not in that place describe the manner of Jesus' appearance. He simply says he "appeared" to all those named.

More than likely the gospel of Mark originally ended with the report of the empty tomb (16:1-8) and only implied a future appearance of the risen Jesus. Matthew, Luke, John, and Paul, however, report that Jesus appeared to Peter and the other disciples. All four gospels specifically mention the women and emphasize they were the ones who first discovered that Jesus was risen. They agree that the tomb was empty.

The Gospels take great care to avoid misunderstandings of Jesus' resurrection, such as that he was a "ghost" (Luke 24:36-43) or had not really died (John 20:19, 26). According to all the sources, Easter faith did not come into being because the tomb was empty, but through encounters with the living Lord. The evidence of the empty tomb alone would have been ambiguous. Those who opposed the Christians recognized that the body could have been stolen or exchanged (Matt. 28:13). The Gospels underscore both the reality and the mystery of Christ's resurrection.

Perhaps the strongest evidence the Gospels present to support the resurrection of Jesus is that the event took the disciples completely by surprise. Their first reactions were of fear instead of joy. What is more, they were so overwhelmed by what they experienced that they came out of hiding and began publicly to proclaim the resurrection of Jesus. If the story of the resurrection was made up by the disciples, it is hard to understand why they would have risked their lives for a message they knew to be false. They had the courage to take that message wherever God led them.

Summary

● Jesus announced that "the time is fulfilled, and the kingdom of God is at hand."

● Jesus' preaching was given credibility by the consistency between his words and his actions.

● Jesus' signs, like his words, proclaimed the imminent approach of God's kingdom.

● Jesus intended his circle of disciples to be the foundation of God's new people.

● Jesus proclaimed himself to be the one through whom God's kingdom was coming.

● The entire New Testament is filled with the certainty that Jesus rose from the grave.

For reflection

Very early on the first day of the week they went to the tomb when the sun had risen. And they were saying to one another, "Who will roll away the stone for us from the door of the tomb?" And looking up, they saw that the stone was rolled back—it was very large. And entering the tomb, they saw a young man sitting on the right side, dressed in a white robe; and they were amazed. And he said to them, "Do not be amazed; you seek Jesus of Nazareth, who was crucified. He has risen, he is not here; see the place where they laid him. But go, tell his disciples and Peter that he is going before you to Galilee; there you will see him, as he told you." And they went out and fled from the tomb; for trembling and astonishment had come upon them; and they said nothing to any one, for they were afraid.

Mark 16:2-8

Christ Jesus lay in death's strong bands
For our offenses given;
But now at God's right hand he stands
And brings us life from heaven.
Therefore let us joyful be
And sing to God right thankfully
Loud songs of hallelujah!

Martin Luther (1483-1546)
Lutheran Book of Worship 134

Christ is with those of humble mind, not with those
who exalt themselves over his flock. The sceptre of the
majesty of God, that is, our Lord Jesus Christ, did not
come with the pride of pretension and arrogance—
though he had the power—but in humility of mind
. . . .

Clement of Rome (c. 30-100)
The Early Christian Fathers
(Oxford, 1956), p. 39

It is correct to say that the culmination of Jesus'
life consists in his death on the cross. But his death
on the cross actually began with the temptation in the
wilderness where Jesus turned back the vision of a
life devoted to his own gain and elected instead a
life of service to others. The same death occurs, bit

by bit, in all his works. If he continues to do the kind of things he had chosen to do, it is clear that the cross will be the end.

Gustaf Wingren
Credo
(Augsburg, 1981), p. 94

From my youth onwards I have found in Jesus my great brother. . . . My own fraternally open relationship with him has grown ever stronger and clearer, and today I see him more strongly and clearly than ever before. I am more than ever certain that a great place belongs to him in Israel's history of faith and that this place cannot be described by any of the usual categories.

Martin Buber (1878-1965)
Two Types of Faith
(Harper & Row, 1961), p. 12

Matthew, Mark, Luke, and John
four men squat around the mat
on which I lie,
and pray,
and sleep.
Night comes,
sleep comes.

Dear Lord Jesus, come.
Four men
have told me this story.
Your story.
Two sit at the foot,
two at the head.
They carry me to you,
Lord Jesus Christ,
when the last breath
beats against my tired lips.
Amen.

African prayer, Fritz Pawelzik, ed.
I Lie on My Mat and Pray
(© 1964 by Friendship Press), p. 9
Used by permission.

12

Jesus in the Creed

The basic confession of the New Testament is that the Lord Jesus is alive and active. The apostles were convinced that God had raised him from the dead. He was the living Lord, and he continued to speak to his people. He spoke to them and revealed himself to them through the Old Testament Scriptures, his teachings, stories told about him, and apostolic preaching and teaching. Even though we look primarily at the New Testament for a picture of Jesus, we should also look at later Christian confessions about him.

One of the most important early statements of faith is the Apostles' Creed. Even though this creed was not actually written by the apostles, it is very old and its statements agree with apostolic teaching. It developed in connection with the rite of Baptism, during which new believers were asked three questions: "Do you believe in God the Father? Do you believe in Jesus Christ, the Son of God? Do you believe in God the Holy Spirit?" The responses to these questions formed the basis for the three articles of the Apostles' Creed.

The Creed is many things:

- a song of praise to God
- an affirmation of agreement with the faith of the apostles
- a rejection of all other lords and powers
- a clear statement of the content of the Christian faith
- a pledge of commitment

The Apostles' Creed continues to be a vital touchstone for believers. When Christians today join in this confession, they identify themselves with the faith expressed in these same words down through the centuries. In their confession of the Second Article, which deals with Jesus Christ, Christians state who it is they believe Jesus was and is.

1. "I believe in Jesus Christ, his only Son, our Lord"

The oldest Christian confession may well be a phrase used in the common celebrations of the first Christian congregations in Palestine: "Maranatha!" (1 Cor. 16:22). This is a confession of the resurrected and present Lord ("Our Lord is here!") as well as a prayer for his return ("Our Lord come!"). The confession of Jesus as Lord is the oldest and most basic Christian confession.

To say that Jesus is Lord is to say he is the ruler of

all things. He is above every power in heaven and on earth. To call Jesus "the Christ" (*Messiah* or "anointed one") means the same thing as calling him the Lord. He is God's King. Yet Jesus' kingship did not conform to the popular expectations of Israel. He was a king who took the path of suffering. "Was it not necessary that the Christ should suffer these things and enter into his glory?" (Luke 24:26) Jesus went to the cross as a paradoxical Messiah, a Christ held up to ridicule. The mocking inscription on the cross reflected this irony: "Jesus of Nazareth, the King of the Jews" (John 19:19).

Rulers in the ancient world were referred to as "sons" of their god. "You are my son; this day I have begotten you" (Ps. 2:7) was a word of divine affirmation shouted to the king of Israel by the people at the time of his coronation. The grandeur of Psalm 2 admittedly did not match the political realities of the time; Israel was not a world power, and its king could scarcely be considered a mighty ruler. This coronation Psalm came to be seen as a promise that God would one day send a king who would truly be his son and rule the world with power and glory.

The Christian community believes Jesus fulfilled this promise. It calls Jesus the Son of God because God has appointed him to rule with authority and establish freedom for God's people. He is a king who reverses all the usual ideas about authority and power. He is a king who accepted powerlessness and was

condemned to death. Behind this bold confession lies
the assurance that God himself affirmed Jesus' kingship by raising him from the dead.

As God's Son, Jesus lives in complete unity with his
Father. Through his words and deeds, through his life
and death, indeed through his whole person, we come
to recognize who God is. "He who has seen me has
seen the Father" (John 14:9). In order to underscore
this particular and unique relationship between Father
and Son, the Creed speaks of Jesus as God's "only"
Son. Through his only Son, God reveals himself as a
loving God. In the face of Christ we see the face of
God.

2. "He was conceived by the power of the Holy Spirit and born of the virgin Mary"

Matthew and Luke are the only gospels that tell us
something about Jesus' life before he began his public
ministry. The stories in Matthew 1-2 and Luke 1-2 are
closely connected with the church's confession of who
Jesus is. They are not told simply as information
(Jesus' youth and early adulthood are largely ignored). The stories of Jesus' birth say something
about the church's faith in him.

Mary, his mother, was a woman of the people.
There was nothing to suggest she would be the
mother of a king. God works through even the most
ordinary of persons. The statement that Mary was

still a virgin when Jesus was born says something about his unique relationship to God and his unique mission. Through his Spirit—that is, the same power by which he called the world into being (Genesis 1)— God initiated a new beginning for all humanity. In Jesus, God joins us. Therefore the church not only speaks of Jesus as being truly human but immediately adds and confesses with equal emphasis that he is truly God. "Conceived by the power of the Holy Spirit" says the Creed.

The church has fought against any understanding of Jesus that would remove either his full humanity or his full divinity. In our day, the identity of Jesus as God is in danger more than his identity as a human being. Only as both God and a man can Jesus both identify with us and save us.

The church gives Mary a place of great honor in its confession of faith. She was chosen by God to have a relationship of special closeness with Jesus. Yet at times her role has been overemphasized. Luke's gospel tells us that one day a woman told Jesus, "Blessed is the womb that bore you, and the breasts that you sucked!" Jesus replied, "Blessed rather are those who hear the word of God and keep it!" (Luke 11:27-28) This description fits Mary perfectly! She was portrayed as a model hearer of God's word, the "handmaiden of the Lord" who humbly accepted God's will (Luke 1:46-48). She is an example for all of someone who remained open and receptive to God's grace.

3. "He suffered under Pontius Pilate, was crucified, died, and was buried"

We can't help but wonder why the Creed has nothing to say about Jesus' public ministry. Speaking of everything that happened between his birth and death, it says only that "he suffered." Does it consider his life unimportant? Actually it concentrates on the essential spirit of his life. The entire path of Jesus, not only his death on the cross, was a road of suffering.

The name of Pontius Pilate ties the death of Jesus to history. Jesus was not a mythological figure created by the church. He was a real person who suffered and died in a particular corner of the Roman Empire during a particular time. The history of Jesus is bound up with human history. The Creed says Jesus was buried. His death was not a hoax. The Son of God actually died and was buried.

4. "He descended into hell"

With this statement, those who first confessed the Apostles' Creed probably had in mind the realm of the dead, or "Hades." One modern version of the Creed reads, "He descended to the dead" (ICET). In the Old Testament the realm of the dead *(Sheol)* was thought of as a depressing place, full of shadows and without the joy of life with God. By saying that Jesus entered the realm of the dead, the church confesses

that Jesus conquered the power of death. He showed
himself to be Lord over both the living and the dead
(Rom. 14:9).

5. "On the third day he rose again"

The Christian faith stands or falls with the resurrection of Jesus. "If Christ has not been raised, then
our preaching is in vain and your faith is in vain"
(1 Cor. 15:14). Jesus' resurrection is the bedrock
foundation of the church. The resurrection means:

- God has reconciled the world to himself.
- God has created new life that is no longer sub-
ject to death.
- The risen Christ is alive and active in his church.

The Christian faith revolves around the message
that Jesus suffered, died, was buried, and was raised
on our behalf.

6. "He ascended into heaven, and is seated at the right hand of the Father"

The "ascension" refers to the last appearance of the
resurrected Christ to his disciples. From now on they
would no longer see him, but experience his presence
in a new way—in the power of the Holy Spirit, in the
communion of the church, in the joyful message of
the gospel, and in the visible signs of the sacraments.

Jesus' ascension did not take him to outer space, where an astronaut could see him. Instead, he entered the hidden realm of God that is everywhere. Heaven ought not be misunderstood as a geographic location. There is no conflict between the belief that Jesus is with God and the belief that he also is alive and working in the world. The resurrected Christ is with God and participates in God's rule and universal presence.

In the ancient world the chief official of a king sat at his right hand. This is the meaning of "seated at the right hand of the Father." The risen Christ has authority over all of God's creation. He rules over every other power in the universe.

7. "He will come again to judge the living and the dead"

Jesus Christ, Lord of the present, is also Lord of the future. At the end of this world and of time, he whose rule is now hidden will come to rule in power and glory. He will judge the world, revealing all that has taken place in history and calling all people to give an account of themselves. The powers of evil will be completely conquered and Christ will bring to perfection all that he has already begun.

The idea that Christ will judge us can be frightening. All our masks will be removed and the truth about ourselves will be made plain. Yet we must realize that *Christ* is the judge. He does not pronounce a verdict based on a cold principle of retribution. Our judge is the same one who loved us enough to give himself for us. On the cross he himself assumed God's judgment on our sin. We will not be judged on the basis of our faults but by the grace of God in Jesus Christ.

Summary

- The confession of Jesus as Lord is the oldest and most basic Christian confession.
- The church has fought against any understanding of Jesus that would remove either his full humanity or his full divinity.
- Jesus showed himself to be Lord over both the living and the dead.
- The Christian faith stands or falls with the resurrection of Jesus.
- The resurrected Christ is with God and participates in God's rule and universal presence.
- We will not be judged on the basis of our faults but by the grace of God in Jesus Christ.

For reflection

Let each of you look not only to his own interests, but also to the interests of others. Have this mind among yourselves, which is yours in Christ Jesus, who, though he was in the form of God, did not count equality with God a thing to be grasped, but emptied himself, taking the form of a servant, being born in the

likeness of men. And being found in human form he
humbled himself and became obedient unto death,
even death on a cross. Therefore God has highly
exalted him and bestowed on him the name which is
above every name, that at the name of Jesus every
knee should bow, in heaven and on earth and under
the earth, and every tongue confess that Jesus Christ
is Lord, to the glory of God the Father.

Phil. 2:4-11

Turn a deaf ear to any speaker who avoids mention
of Jesus Christ who was of David's line, born of
Mary, who was truly born, ate and drank; was truly
persecuted under Pontius Pilate, truly crucified and
died while those in heaven, on earth, and under the
earth beheld it; who also was truly raised from the
dead, the Father having raised him, who in like
manner will raise us also who believe in him—his
Father, I say, will raise us in Christ Jesus, apart from
whom we have not true life.

Ignatius (1st-2nd centuries)
The Early Christian Fathers
(Oxford, 1956), pp. 60-61

God became man, and it was the Lord himself who
saved us.

Irenaeus (c. 130-200)
The Early Christian Fathers
(Oxford, 1956), pp. 60-61

God died! If this does not astonish us, what will?
The church must keep this astonishment alive. The
church ceases to exist when she loses this astonishment. . . . The person astonished by the tidings "God
has died" can no longer be astonished at anything
else.

Kazoh Kitamori
What Asian Christians Are Thinking
(New Day, 1976), p. 207

To say Jesus Christ rose from the dead is to say
that he reigns as Lord. There may be more which can
be said but it may not be necessary to say more.
But to say this *is* necessary.

Kent S. Knutson (1924-1973)
Gospel, Church, Mission
(Augsburg, 1976), p. 54

Lord Jesus Christ,
the only Son
Of God, creation's author,

Redeemer of your wand'ring ones,
And source of all true pleasure:
O Lamb of God,
O Lord divine,
Conform our lives to your design,
And on us all have mercy.
Amen.

Nikolaus Decius (1490-1541)
Lutheran Book of Worship 166

13

Jesus Our Savior

The preaching of the apostles centered on what God has done for human beings through the death and resurrection of Jesus. God has taken the initiative to reconcile us to himself. Through Jesus Christ he has freed us from the power of sin and brought us into a new relationship with him. This is the central message of the New Testament:

God shows his love for us in that while we were yet sinners Christ died for us. Since, therefore, we are now justified by his blood, much more shall we be saved by him from the wrath of God. For if while we were enemies we were reconciled to God by the death of his Son, much more, now that we are reconciled, shall we be saved by his life. Not only so, but we also rejoice in God through our Lord Jesus Christ, through whom we have now received our reconciliation (Rom. 5:8-11).

1. The God who is for us

The New Testament contains many statements about the meaning of Jesus' death and resurrection. One phrase, however, summarizes them all: In Jesus

God was "for us." God has loved us by giving us the ultimate gift—himself. The cross is the sign of his unconditional love for us.

Many stories in the Gospels, even though they may not mention Jesus' death, reveal the kind of love and acceptance he brought to people. The story about the woman caught in adultery is a good example:

The scribes and the Pharisees brought a woman who had been caught in adultery, and placing her in the midst they said to him, "Teacher, this woman has been caught in the act of adultery. Now in the law Moses commanded us to stone such. What do you say about her?" This they said to test him, that they might have some charge to bring against him. Jesus bent down and wrote with his finger on the ground. And as they continued to ask him, he stood up and said to them, "Let him who is without sin among you be the first to throw a stone at her." And once more he bent down and wrote with his finger on the ground. But when they heard it, they went away, one by one, beginning with the eldest, and Jesus was left alone with the woman standing before him. Jesus looked up and said to her, "Woman, where are they? Has no one condemned you?" She said, "No one, Lord." And Jesus said, "Neither do I condemn you; go, and do not sin again" (John 8:3-11).

Jesus consistently brought a forgiving and transforming presence to people caught in the power and guilt of sin. (See also Mark 2:13-17; Luke 7:36-50; 19:1-10). He made a sharp distinction between how God judges those who confess their sins and those who are self-righteous:

He also told this parable to some who trusted in themselves that they were righteous and despised others: "Two men went up into the temple to pray, one a Pharisee and the other a tax collector. The Pharisee stood and prayed thus with himself, 'God, I thank thee that I am not like other men, extortioners, unjust, adulterers, or even like this tax collector. I fast twice a week, I give tithes of all that I get.' But the tax collector, standing far off, would not even lift up his eyes to heaven, but beat his breast, saying, 'God, be merciful to me a sinner!' I tell you, this man went down to his house justified rather than the other; for every one who exalts himself will be humbled, but he who humbles himself will be exalted" (Luke 18:9-14).

Jesus had little patience with self-righteous persons. His message to the proud and conceited was always severe, yet his mercy toward the humble and the oppressed was complete. This mercy came to a climax in Jesus' obedient death on our behalf. His faithfulness revealed a God who is faithful, who loves us and is for us.

2. The biblical doctrine of justification

In the parable about the Pharisee and the tax collector, Jesus used a word that is very important for the Christian faith: *justification*. The Bible uses this word to describe the relationship between human beings and God. Those who live in a right relationship with God are said to be "justified" in God's eyes.

The concept of justification is rooted in the Old Testament's understanding of justice. In an act of undeserved love, God established Israel as his chosen people. God saved them from slavery in Egypt, revealed his will to them, and gave them a promise of land and a future. In return, his people committed themselves to serve him alone and keep his commandments. They would love their neighbors as themselves and exercise justice in the land God had given them. Our notion of "tempering justice with mercy" is different from the concept of justice in the Old Testament. Mercy was not contrasted with justice. Justice was seen not as a cold retribution for evil but as an expression of righteousness and mercy. God showed his justice not only by judging his people, but by establishing them as his own possession among all the nations.

The story of human sin is the story of our rebellion against God and against the role he has given us. We are not satisfied to receive his gifts and practice mercy and justice. We place ourselves first, before God.

The New Testament confesses that God has acted decisively through Jesus Christ to establish justice once again. In Christ God is establishing a new relationship with people that is deeper and more comprehensive than the relationship he established with

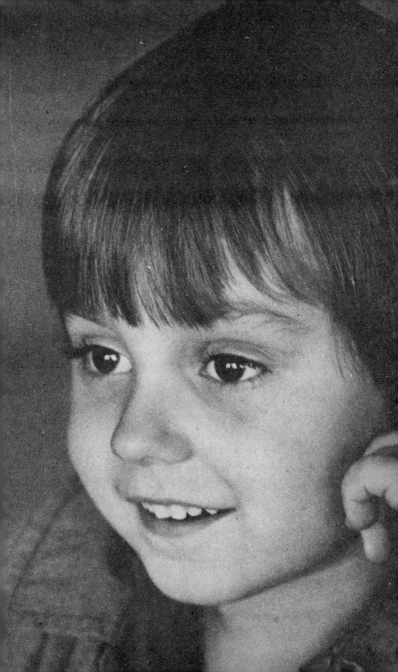

Israel. Jesus did not ignore our sin or God's judgment
on our sin. Instead, he took both our sin and God's
judgment of it on himself. In a way that defies all
understanding, Jesus established justice once more
by becoming a once-and-for-all sacrifice for all human
sin. In words and actions, through the cross and his
resurrection, Jesus made it possible for all human
beings to come into a new and just relationship with
God, to be "justified."

The apostle Paul provides the most detailed pre-
sentation of the doctrine of justification in the New
Testament. His letters to the Romans and the Gala-
tians, in particular, are powerful statements of this
most central Christian theme.

The letter to the Philippians provides an insight
into Paul's background in Judaism and his understanding of justification:

If any other man thinks he has reason for confidence in
the flesh, I have more: circumcised on the eighth day, of
the people of Israel, of the tribe of Benjamin, a Hebrew
born of Hebrews; as to the law a Pharisee, as to zeal a
persecutor of the church, as to righteousness under the
law blameless (3:4-6).

Paul was taught to believe that righteousness before
God could be established through obedience to the
Jewish law. After encountering Christ, it became
clear to him that moral behavior—however good or
impressive—could not reestablish a broken relation-

ship with God. It is not only outward sin that separates us from God; so also does self-centered pride in our own pious achievements:

> But whatever gain I had, I counted as loss for the sake of Christ. Indeed I count everything as loss because of the surpassing worth of knowing Jesus Christ my Lord (Phil. 3:7-8).

Paul's understanding of justification revolves around God's grace. Grace is undeserved love. We human beings cannot restore ourselves to a right relationship with God through our own actions. God himself justifies us, by grace, for Christ's sake, through faith. Justification is God's gift that cannot be earned, but only received. This is the "gospel," the good news.

The New Testament uses various images to describe the fact that Jesus Christ assumed God's judgment on the entire human race. For example, Paul uses the word *redemption*. The language of "redemption" offers one metaphor among many others. Over the centuries theologians expanded these images and themes into "theories of the atonement," explanations of how we are brought back into a relationship with God. No one explanation or theory succeeds in probing the mystery and significance of Christ's atonement. Each, in its own way, expresses the good news that God *has* justified sinners through the death and resurrection of Jesus.

3. Luther's interpretation of justification

Martin Luther's role as a church reformer began with his personal experience of the grace of God. During his early years in an Augustinian monastery he was oppressed by the image of Jesus as a righteous judge who wanted only to condemn him for his sins. Eventually, through his study of the Scriptures, Luther realized the righteousness of God is not just something God *demands,* but also something God *creates* through faith. This insight became the foundation of all his later preaching, teaching, and writing. The righteousness of God is an active righteousness that justifies sinners.

The distinction between the righteousness that God demands and the righteousness that God creates lies behind the terms "law" and "gospel" that occur so frequently in Luther's writings. The focus of his theology was on the proper distinction between the law (that reveals our sinful nature) and the gospel (the good news that God has taken our sin on himself in Christ).

For Luther, the gospel was never just a concept *about* what God has done. The gospel is the living proclamation of what God has done *for us.* The gospel is a powerful word that destroys our old nature and recreates us in the image of Christ. This gospel comes to us first and foremost through the preaching of God's Word. The proclaimed Word creates faith in the hearer (Rom. 10:17). Through Baptism into Christ we are united to him, "so that as Christ was raised from the dead by the glory of the Father, we too might walk in newness of life" (Rom. 6:4).

The doctrine of justification has always been open to misunderstanding. The concept that God freely removes all human guilt strikes some people as being irresponsible. What incentive is left for moral behavior if all sin is forgiven? Paul reacted strongly to such charges: "Are we to continue in sin that grace may abound? By no means! How can we who died to sin still live in it?" (Rom. 6:1-2) Luther guarded against such a misunderstanding of the gospel by emphasizing the radical nature of justification. God does not just see us *as* righteous, but actually begins a process by which he *makes* us righteous through faith. God is creating us to be new creatures in the image of his Son. Christ himself is at work in our lives, producing the fruits of faith.

4. Interpreting justification today

It has been suggested that the doctrine of justification no longer applies to the concerns of modern people. Unlike the late Middle Ages, when Luther struggled to find a gracious God, our time does not emphasize the themes of sin and grace. The very notion of sin is often said to be old-fashioned and out-of-date.

The church's message concerning justification has also suffered from overly-literal explanations of how Christ has atoned for human sin. When metaphors

and images of the atonement are taken too concrete-
ly, they distort our understanding of God. For example, God has sometimes been seen as paying a
debt to the devil, or as requiring the bloody sacrifice of his Son in order to satisfy his wrath. When
such language is used it often contradicts other things
we know about God from the Scriptures, including
his power over evil and his steadfast love and forgiveness.

If the church is to make the message of justification
known to people today, it must interpret the doctrine
in a way that is both faithful to God's revelation of
himself and meaningful in our current context.

Society as a whole may be little concerned about sin
or God's will, but people still understand the gospel.
All human beings are God's creatures, and all have
the same basic needs. No matter how much our culture changes, we will always need the love of God
and the fulfillment that comes from being faithful
to his will. It may be that we cannot matter-of-factly
repeat the phrases used by Paul or Luther. Yet that
should not surprise us. We would not expect modern
people to understand what we say about God if we
were to speak to them using ancient Greek. Why
then should we expect them to respond to images
and symbols drawn from a culture very distant from
their own experiences? If the doctrine of justification
is to be understood today, it must be expressed in
language that communicates something to people
living in today's world.

Sin may be an unpopular word, but we all know the meaning of the term *slavery*. We experience slavery to our mistakes, our desires, our jobs, and even other people. We can be enslaved by government repression or by a destructive self-image. We can be enslaved by the constant need to build ourselves up in the eyes of others. We can be enslaved by the need always to rationalize our actions, to accept ourselves and be accepted by others.

The desire to be someone, to count for something, is like a hidden motor that drives us. It lies concealed behind our striving for recognition, status, and affluence. Surrounded by all the impressive products of our technologically sophisticated world, we are still dependent on a simple "gospel" word from another human being. We need someone to love us for who we really are.

On a much deeper level, all of us are dependent on the gospel word from God that affirms our whole existence as persons. The gospel has the power to recreate us in his image, to free us from our slavery to ourselves. It places us in a new relationship with him and with other human beings.

In Jesus Christ, all of us who strive for affirmation find a God who is seeking and pursuing us in love. Christ speaks to us and says, "I accept you the way you are." He breaks through our defenses and opens us to the future.

The message of justification is not outdated. It needs to be proclaimed today as never before.

Summary

● God has taken the initiative and restored us to a relationship with himself through the death and resurrection of Jesus Christ.

● Jesus' faithfulness revealed a God who is faithful, who loves us and is for us.

● Those who live in a right relationship with God are said to be "justified" in God's eyes.

● Jesus did not ignore our sin or God's judgment on our sin. Instead, he took both our sin and God's judgment of it on himself.

● Justification is God's gift that cannot be earned, but only received. This is the "gospel," the good news.

● The gospel has the power to recreate us in God's image and free us from our slavery to ourselves.

For reflection

Therefore, since we are justified by faith, we have peace with God through our Lord Jesus Christ. Through him we have obtained access to this grace in which we stand, and we rejoice in our hope of sharing the glory of God. . . .

Since, therefore, we are now justified by his blood, much more shall we be saved by him from the wrath of God. For if while we were enemies we were reconciled to God by the death of his Son, much more, now that we are reconciled, shall we be saved by his life. Not only so, but we also rejoice in God through our Lord Jesus Christ, through whom we have now received our reconciliation.

Rom. 5:1-2, 9-11

There's a wideness in God's mercy,
Like the wideness of the sea;
There's a kindness in his justice
Which is more than liberty.
There is no place where earth's sorrows
Are more felt than up in heav'n.
There is no place where earth's failings
Have such kindly judgment giv'n.

Frederick W. Faber (1814-1863)
Lutheran Book of Worship 290

We also, who have been called in Christ Jesus through his will, are not justified through ourselves or through our own wisdom or understanding or piety, or our actions done in holiness of heart, but through faith, for it is through faith that Almighty God has justified all men that have been from the beginning of time: to whom be glory for ever and ever. Amen.

Clement of Rome (c. 30-100)
The Early Christian Fathers
(Oxford, 1956), p. 41

It is this that we can learn from Christ. The more fully one is aware of his own identity, the easier it is for him to let go of himself. His hands do not grasp vice-like that portion of existence which has come his way. Since he has experienced and can call the fullness of life eternal his own, he is not out to hold fast. He can open his hands.

Dorothee Sölle
Beyond Mere Obedience
(Augsburg, 1970), p. 73

When I was a child I often had a toothache. . . . And I knew those dentists; I knew they started fiddling about with all sorts of other teeth which had not yet begun to ache. They would not let sleeping dogs lie; if you gave them an inch, they took an ell.

Now, if I may put it that way, Our Lord is like the dentists. If you give Him an inch, He will take an ell. Dozens of people go to Him to be cured of some one particular sin. . . . Well, He will cure it all right: but He will not stop there. That may be all you asked; but if you once call Him in, He will give you the full treatment.

C. S. Lewis (1898-1963)
Mere Christianity
(Macmillan, 1952), p. 171

You who once wandered on earth, leaving foot-
prints which we should follow; You, who still from
your heaven look down upon each wanderer,
strengthen the weary, encourage the despondent, lead
back the erring, comfort the striving; You, who also at
the end of days shall return to judge whether each
person individually has followed you: our God and
Savior, let your example stand clearly before the
eyes of our soul to disperse the mists; strengthen
us that unfalteringly we may keep this before our
eyes, that we by resembling and following you may
later find the way to the judgment, for it is necessary
for every person to be brought to the judgment,
but also through you to be brought to eternal happiness hereafter with you. Amen.

Søren Kierkegaard (1813-1855)
The Gospel of Suffering
(Augsburg, 1948), p. 4, adapted

Part Five

Who Is the Holy Spirit?

The Holy Spirit is not an invisible mystery. He does not correspond to the innermost hiddenness of our being. He is not, by nature, within us. The Spirit comes to us from without, from the outside. (That's always how God comes to us.) He is present for us promising to do his work whenever the Word is read or heard. He is present and working in baptism. He is present and working in and through the Lord's Supper. If we want to be touched by the work of the Holy Spirit we know where to go! We read our Bibles. We listen to the word proclaimed. We get together with God's people. We celebrate our baptism. We participate in the Lord's Supper. We expect God's Spirit to work on us, transforming our lives through these visible and outer signs. That's what we expect. Word and sacraments do not automatically guarantee God's presence. His promise, however, is attached to these outer, visible signs.

Richard A. Jensen
Touched by the Spirit
(Augsburg, 1975), pp. 67-68

14

The Work of the Spirit

In both Greek and Hebrew, the word for "wind" or "breath" can also mean "spirit." The Bible understands the Spirit of God to be much like the wind: "The wind blows where it wills, and you hear the sound of it, but you do not know whence it comes or whither it goes . . ." (John 3:8). The wind cannot be caught or controlled by human beings. It has a power of its own. It cannot be seen with the eyes. Yet the wind has effects, and you can see the things it does. The Holy Spirit defies human understanding or control, and cannot be seen. Yet the Spirit is the power of God at work in the world.

When we speak of the Spirit we are expressing a particular point of view concerning the nature and activity of God. God is not a solitary being, aloof and uninvolved with the world. He moves beyond himself, he exceeds all limitations, he establishes communion with human beings.

1. The biblical view of the Spirit

The Old Testament understands God's Spirit to be creative and powerful. God speaks, and by the power of his Spirit his will is done (Gen. 1:1-3; Pss. 33:6; 104: 29-30). The Spirit works through nature and through human beings. The Spirit is the source of human powers and skills (Exod. 31:3; 35:31).

Through the power of God's Spirit, heroes in Israel's history accomplished great deeds (Judg. 6:34; 14:6). The Spirit is the bringer of forgiveness, life, and salvation (Ps. 51:10-12; Isa. 63:10-14; Hag. 2:4-5). He is the source of prophetic inspiration (Num. 24: 2-3; 1 Sam. 10:6, 10; 19:20; 2 Sam. 23:2; Isa. 48:16; 61:1; Zech. 7:12). The Spirit is also the power of God that will one day bring creation to completion. In the future the Spirit will come in a new way, creating new life and righteousness (Isa. 11:2-9; 32:15-17; 42:1-4; 44:3; Ezek. 36:26-27; 39:29; Joel 2:28).

The four gospels agree that the Holy Spirit was present in Jesus in a special and unique way. The Spirit was involved in Jesus' birth, baptism, and ministry. Jesus promised his disciples that after he was gone the Spirit would be present with them as the "Counselor" (John 14:16-18). The Spirit is the continuing presence of Jesus that remains with his disciples forever and leads them into all truth (John 16:13).

On the Day of Pentecost the Holy Spirit was poured out on the disciples, empowering them to proclaim the gospel boldly (Acts 1-2). The same Spirit that had spoken through the Old Testament prophets and was uniquely present in Jesus was now given through Jesus to the church.

The Spirit is received by faith, delivers believers from idolatry and slavery to false lords, and leads to the confession that Jesus is Lord (1 Cor. 12:2-3; Gal. 3:14). The Spirit gives power to the proclamation of the gospel (Rom. 15:18-19; 1 Cor. 2:3-4; 1 Thess. 1:5). The Spirit is the source of new freedom and life (Rom. 7:6). Christians are led by the Spirit (Rom. 8:14), which means they are to walk according to the Spirit and not some other standard (Rom. 8:4; Gal. 5:16). The Spirit produces the fruits of love, joy, peace, patience, kindness, goodness, faithfulness, gentleness, self-control, and righteousness (Rom. 14:17; Gal. 5:2-24; Phil. 4:7). Through the Spirit's work the powers of sin and death are defeated (Rom. 8:2). The Holy Spirit is the source of spiritual gifts given to each believer, the greatest of which is love (1 Corinthians 12-13).

The work of the Holy Spirit is as broad as the power and activity of God. The Spirit is the creative, redemptive, and sustaining power of God at work throughout all creation. God's Spirit is active in the lives of individuals, of communities and nations, and in nature. The Spirit is God in action. The Spirit works through the gospel, calling people to faith in Jesus Christ. Both the ability to believe and the ability to love are gifts of the Holy Spirit. The Spirit desires

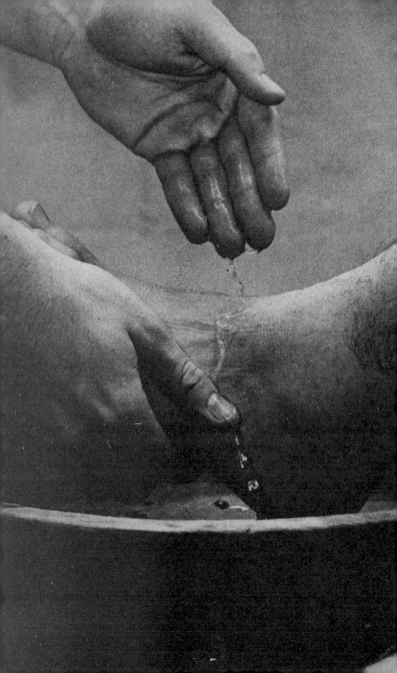

to transform human lives and the structures of community life and renew every aspect of creation.

The process of being transformed by God's Spirit is a dynamic one in which all our powers and will are challenged. Yet the actual change that is accomplished is a gift. We seek to be open to the Spirit's work, yet we know that even our desire to be open is the work of the Spirit.

The rich variety of the Spirit's work is indicated by words like *vocation, cleansing, regeneration, election, illumination, conversion, justification,* and *sanctification*. God is at work through the Spirit to reconcile the world to himself. He accomplishes this through the gospel of Jesus Christ. The close connection between the work of the Spirit and the effects of the gospel is illustrated by words such as *life, love, liberty, power, unity,* and *fellowship*. The Spirit is at work in human relationships, bringing about that harmony of will and purpose that God intends for all people.

According to the Bible, it is God's intention to establish a faithful people. Individuals are supported by the community of believers. Any Christian can fall into despondency and doubt, trouble or temptation. Christians pray for each other, comfort each other, and accept and bear with each other. The church is intended to be a caring community that extends God's love into the world. The church, as the community of faith, is the work of the Spirit.

God is active through the Spirit in a multitude of ways: in the joy that comes from an individual's relationship with the Creator; in the caring, comforting, and supportive relationships between family members and friends; in the realization of forgiveness between people who have long been enemies; in the willingness of a proud person to confess his or her fault to another; and in all realizations of freedom, integrity, compassion, competence, justice, reconciliation, and joy. The Holy Spirit is God at work in all things, bringing about his will.

2. The doctrine of the Trinity

The Christian faith speaks about God the Father, God the Son, and God the Holy Spirit. This language sometimes raises questions about whether Christians believe in more than one God or in a divided God.

The teaching that describes the relationship among Father, Son, and Holy Spirit is the doctrine of the Trinity. This doctrine has been called illogical, incomprehensible, and far removed from simple faith in God. Yet this teaching developed out of the basic New Testament understanding of God. It reflects the biblical view of the Father, Son, and Holy Spirit, even though "the Trinity" is not a New Testament term.

The Gospels point out the intimate relationship between Jesus and his Father (Matt. 11:27; Luke 12:8-9). The early Christians were convinced that in Jesus, God himself was with them (Matt. 1:22-23; John 1:1-18; 14:8-9). The identity of Jesus is very important for the church. If Jesus is only a human being, then no matter how noble he was, he would not have been able to free human beings from the powers of sin and death. Yet if Jesus is also God, does that mean there are two Gods? And if the Spirit is truly the presence of Jesus with the church, does that make three Gods?

Standing in the tradition of Jewish monotheism, the Christian church asserts its belief in one God. Yet there is a "threefold character" to God's presence among us as Creator, Redeemer, and Sanctifier. The unity of God is known in and through the divine presence expressed in the New Testament as Father, Son, and Holy Spirit.

The doctrine of the Trinity expresses faith in one God, together with the conviction that God is three-fold. It makes formal the message of unity and trinity that is clearly implied in the Scriptures. Christian faith is directed to the one God who is triune.

3. The nature of the church

The New Testament uses many different images to describe the church (see, for example, 1 Cor. 3:9; Eph. 2:21-22; 5:25-27; 1 Tim. 3:15; 1 Peter 2:5; Rev. 19:7). In 1 Corinthians 12, Paul describes the church as a body with many members. The church is *like* a body, because each member needs the others. Yet the church also *is* a body. It is the body of Christ. All Christians are united in the one body of the risen Christ (1 Cor. 10:16-17). Believers live with Christ in a real, personal communion established through the gospel.

The New Testament also describes the church as the people of God. The church is both a continuation of Israel and the recipient of a new covenant (Rom. 11:12-24; 2 Cor. 3:6). Like Israel, the church:

- has been chosen and called by God
- was not chosen for its own sake but as an instrument of God's will in the world
- lives in history and is not yet perfected
- receives its unity as a gift of God

The Apostles' Creed states, "I believe in the Holy Spirit, the holy catholic Church. . . ." The church is the creation of the Holy Spirit. It is both "holy" and "catholic." According to the Bible, everything that belongs to God is holy. The church is holy because it belongs to God and lives under his forgiveness. Yet Christians are also imperfect and sinful. They are both saints and sinners at the same time.

The contradictions between the conduct of Christians and the message they proclaim has been a problem for the church since its earliest years. There have been many attempts to exclude obvious sinners from the community of believers in order to form a community that deserves the name "holy." Yet sin goes much deeper than external behavior. All attempts to create a completely "pure" church have failed. Only God has the power to do that, and the perfection of

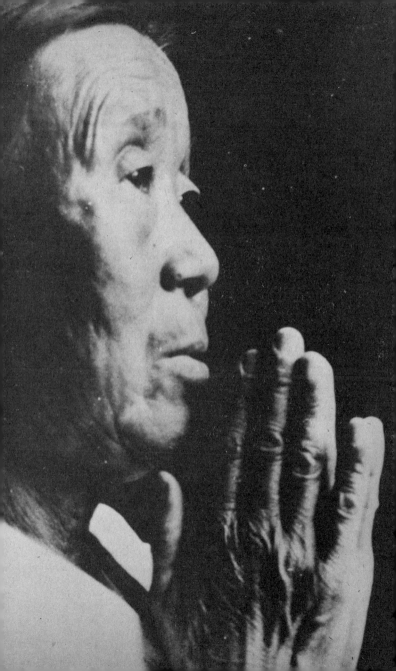

the church lies in his hands. The church is a place where God is communing with sinners, even as he is transforming them into the image of his Son.

Because Christians believe in one Lord, the church is by nature one, or catholic. The word *catholic* comes from a Greek word meaning "related to the whole." It expresses the truth that the church is universal. The people of God reach across all national, racial, and class barriers. The gospel is intended for all and unites all into one body.

The spiritual unity of the church exists in spite of divisions in the church. This unity seeks visible expression. The unity of the church does not demand one comprehensive organization, but it does imply fellowship in the proclamation of the gospel, in the celebration of the sacraments, and in carrying out Christ's mission. We are not under obligation to create the unity of the church. The church is one and cannot be divided (1 Cor. 1:10-13). It is, however, our task to realize more and more the unity that is already a fact in Christ.

The most pressing reason for making every effort toward full expression of unity is the church's mission in the world. Jesus, praying not only for his disciples but also for us, said, "I do not pray for these only, but also for those who believe in me through their word, that they may all be one; even as thou, Father, art in me, and I in thee, that they also may be in us, so that the world may believe that thou hast sent me" (John 17:20-21).

Though the church is not of this world, it still lives and works in this world. It shares in the world's sin and imperfection. Separation, disunity, dissension, and division are constant threats that must be overcome. Separatism within the church is a sin. Where this exists, Christians have no other option than to confess their guilt and repent. Some divisions within the church also have the dimension of particular interpretations of the faith. For example, the Protestant Reformers of the 16th century became convinced that they could preserve the true preaching of the gospel only in separation from the rest of the Catholic Church. Such divisions as these have sometimes been described as "tragic necessities." Under such circumstances only mutual efforts to achieve a correct understanding of the gospel can lead to reconciliation.

The development of denominational pluralism on the American continent is an example of how nontheological factors have contributed to divisions among Christians. Ethnic identities and cultural backgrounds have played an important role. Scandinavian and German Lutherans, Scottish Presbyterians, English Methodists, and Italian Catholics, among others, arrived at different times, settled in different places, and brought with them their own forms of worship and life. Often isolated from one another by great distances, unfamiliar languages and peculiar customs, they have taken decades—even when confessing the same beliefs—to become acquainted with each other.

Only recently have there been serious attempts at mutual understanding and fellowship.

The complexity of the problems that divide the church ought not deter us from seeking a solution. The risen Lord called his disciples out of different backgrounds and sent them into the world together. The very task of proclaiming the gospel in different times and places prevented them from always expressing the good news in the same way. Because of the very mission of the church, Christians are called to express their unity as well as the truth of the gospel.

The ecumenical movement in this century has done much to open the doors to a greater expression of unity among the people of God. Church bodies that have for centuries lived in isolation from each other have now come together with the intention of establishing and deepening their mutual fellowship.

In the ecumenical movement, Christians have learned that unity does not require uniformity, but can be achieved through fellowship in which diversity is possible. Every attempt at uniformity is sure to fail because of the diversity of the world itself. The unity of the church must allow room for various means of proclamation and worship, for different theologies and methods of organization. These variations must, at the same time, actually contribute to the communication of the gospel in a pluralistic world, and must be held together by a common understanding of the gospel.

Summary

● The work of the Holy Spirit is as broad as the power and activity of God. The Spirit is the creative, redemptive, and sustaining power of God at work throughout all of creation.

● The rich variety of the Spirit's work is indicated by words like *vocation, cleansing, regeneration, election, illumination, conversion, justification,* and *sanctification.*

● The doctrine of the Trinity reflects the biblical view of the Father, Son, and Holy Spirit.

● The church is the people of God and the body of Christ.

● The church is holy because it belongs to God and lives under his forgiveness.

● Because Christians believe in one Lord, the church is by nature one, or catholic.

For reflection

For this reason I bow my knees before the Father, from whom every family in heaven and on earth is named, that according to the riches of his glory he may grant you to be strengthened with might through his Spirit in the inner man, and that Christ may dwell in your hearts through faith; that you, being rooted and grounded in love, may have power to comprehend with all the saints what is the breadth and length and height and depth, and to know the love of Christ

which surpasses knowledge, that you may be filled
with all the fulness of God.

   Eph. 3:14-19

Come, Holy Ghost, God and Lord,
With all your graces now outpoured
On each believer's mind and heart;
Your fervent love to them impart.
Lord, by the brightness of your light
In holy faith your Church unite;
From ev'ry land and ev'ry tongue,
This to your praise, O Lord, our God, be sung:
Alleluia! Alleluia!

   Martin Luther (1483-1546)
   Lutheran Book of Worship 163

   The Holy Spirit establishes the righteousness of
heaven in the midst of the unrighteousness of earth
and will not stop or stay until all that is dead has
been brought to life and a new *world* has come into
being.

   Karl Barth (1886-1968)
   The Word of God and the Word of Man
   (Harper & Bros., 1957), p. 50

The nearer we come to Christ's cross, the nearer we come to each other. How can our divisions and our enmities be maintained in the sight of his bitter suffering and death? How, in the light of Christ's "open heart," can we remain closed and fearful about the church?

Jürgen Moltmann
The Passion for Life
(Fortress, 1978), p. 84

What we usually talk about as church is what we have in our power to build. . . . Church as church of Jesus Christ is always created from beyond ourselves, from outside of us. God is always involved in Jesus' creation of the corporate self. What is important is what is being done to us in that God liberates us. We cannot do it. God is always at work destroying our playing church.

Frederick Herzog
Liberation Theology
(Seabury, 1972), p. 195

On your last days on earth
you promised
to leave us the Holy Spirit
as our present comforter.

We also know
that your Holy Spirit blows over this earth.
But we do not understand him.
Many think
he is only wind or a feeling.
Let your Holy Spirit
break into our lives.
Let him come like blood into our veins,
so that we will be driven
entirely by your will.
Let your Spirit
blow over wealthy Europe and America,
so that men there will be humble.
Let him blow over the poor parts of the world,
so that men there need suffer no more.
Let him blow over Africa,
so that men here may understand
what true freedom is.
There are a thousand voices and spirits
in this world,
but we want to hear only your voice,
and be open only to your Spirit.
Amen.

African prayer, Fritz Pawelzik, ed.
I Lie on My Mat and Pray
(© 1964 by Friendship Press), p. 50
Used by permission.

15

The Word of the Gospel

The church draws its very life from the gospel. The gospel is not a human plan or theory, but a powerful, external word of grace spoken by God himself. The gospel calls forth faith, and faith, in turn, trusts God's word. The Holy Spirit works through the gospel to create, sustain, and empower the church.

The means by which the gospel comes to us are the word and the sacraments. The Holy Spirit is able to use such humble things as human language, water, bread, and wine as means of grace. Through word and sacraments we encounter a gracious God and are put into a new relationship with him.

1. The life of the church

The church's life revolves around forgiveness. The Apostles' Creed says, "I believe in the Holy Spirit . . . the communion of saints, the forgiveness of sins. . . ." The church is established by God's forgiveness and continues to live out of that forgiveness. Christians are sinners, yet they are also saints. They have been claimed by God and are being transformed into the image of his Son. The church is a communion of saints that is still in constant need of forgiveness.

Jesus has authorized Christians to forgive sins. Speaking to his disciples, he said, "If you forgive the sins of any, they are forgiven; if you retain the sins of any, they are retained" (John 20:23; see also Matt. 16:18-19; 18:18). Announcing the gospel of God's forgiveness and forgiving the sins of others is part of the ministry that belongs to every Christian. This ministry includes the opportunity and privilege of listening to the troubles of others and consoling them with the promises of God (James 5:16). It is very helpful to hear God's personal word of absolution from the lips of another person we can trust.

The ministry of pastors is related to, and yet distinct from, the ministry of all Christians. Pastors have the specific tasks of preaching and teaching the word of God to the church and presiding over the celebration of the sacraments. Their usual responsibilities also include counseling, visitation, parish administration, and community outreach.

Candidates are appointed to the office of the ministry through the rite of ordination. They are blessed by prayer, and by the laying on of hands by pastors—a reminder that the church is universal and united by its faith in Christ. Pastors promise to preach and teach in accordance with the Holy Scriptures, the Creeds, and the Confessions of the church, to be diligent in worship, study, prayer, and example, and to be faithful witnesses in the world.

In describing the first Christian congregation in Jerusalem, the book of Acts says, "they devoted themselves to the apostles' teaching and fellowship, to the breaking of bread and the prayers" (Acts 2:42). Through the centuries, these same elements have remained central to the life of the church: the word of God, the communion of saints, the sacraments, and prayer.

The traditional word used to describe the church's worship is "liturgy." *Liturgy* literally means "the work of the people." In its broadest sense, it includes everything Christians do out of a grateful response to what God has done for them. We worship God with our entire lives. This is our "liturgy," our "work." In the more narrow sense of the word, *liturgy* refers to the specific orders of worship within Christian congregations.

Worship services are structured around the two essential elements of the preached word and the sacraments. All the other traditional elements of prayer and praise are clustered around these, and can be expanded, compressed, or replaced with alternate forms, depending on the season of the church year and the needs and desires of the congregation.

The sacraments of Baptism and Holy Communion are means of grace by which persons are encountered by Jesus Christ. God is present everywhere, but in the sacraments, as in the word, he is present *for* us and

for our salvation. The Holy Spirit works through the "language" of sacramental action. The Spirit uses earthly things to embrace our whole being with the gospel and God's saving presence.

Some Christian denominations describe their services as "non-liturgical." By this they mean they do not include elements unique to the traditional service of Holy Communion. These elements include the Kyrie, Great Thanksgiving, proper prefaces, and traditional vestments. Yet most congregations develop "liturgies," that is, traditions that vary little from week to week. Most have a set of familiar phrases, prayers, responses, and hymns.

The language used in public worship should have a durable quality and be applicable to widely different types of people. The so-called liturgical churches (Orthodox, Roman Catholic, Lutheran, Episcopal) believe it is important to develop a common liturgical language. In this way congregations can avoid falling into patterns that exclude some people or follow the personal whims of the worship leader or pastor.

The liturgy is an action of the entire worshiping community that can embrace and sustain us. Individuals enter worship services with different moods. Those with family troubles may not be able to sing a hymn of praise with enthusiasm. Those who are overly tired may not be able to concentrate on every word that is spoken. Yet they can still receive the support that comes from the common worship of the Christian community.

In the liturgy we can be immersed in and carried along by the word of God. The liturgy speaks to us with biblical images, parables, and motifs. The language of the liturgy captures and communicates the mystery of salvation. Every outward action during the worship service is but a vessel for the incomprehensible yet effective mystery of God's presence.

2. Preaching and teaching

The church is bound to the word of God in its ministry. God's word is powerful and active. The Holy Spirit uses human words to speak God's word to human hearts.

The Scriptures preserve and convey God's word to people today. Christians read, interpret, and proclaim the message. The church's own authority is always subject to the word of God in the Scriptures. The Bible is the standard by which every proclamation of the church must be judged.

The word *sermon* comes from a Latin word that means proclamation or conversation. The task of a sermon is to make Jesus Christ known: his coming, life, suffering, death, resurrection, and will for us today. The primary goal is to create faith in those who listen. This takes place through the power of the Holy Spirit at work in the hearer.

In order for a sermon to achieve its purpose, it must communicate the gospel of Jesus Christ is a way that is meaningful to those who listen. For this reason pastors must take into account not only the historical and theological background of the Scriptures, but also the language, settings, and needs of people today. The gospel of the risen Lord needs to be communicated in each time and place in a way that is both meaningful and faithful.

Closely related to the task of preaching is that of teaching. Christians need to be taught the content of the Scriptures and the meaning of the gospel in their lives. Jesus placed great emphasis on teaching (Matt. 28:19-20), as did Paul (1 Cor. 12:28). Jesus himself was often called "Teacher." The teaching ministry of the church deserves the best efforts of every Christian and is a special responsibility of pastors.

3. Holy Baptism

The task of baptizing goes hand in hand with the task of proclaiming the gospel. The New Testament teaches that the sacrament of Baptism accomplishes many things, including:

- adoption by God into the family of God
- the forgiveness of sins
- granting of the Holy Spirit
- incorporation into the church

The most conspicuous element at the celebration of a baptism is the human element. Many people are involved: a pastor, the one baptized, parents, sponsors, and the congregation. Yet according to the New Testament, God himself does the baptizing. God works through the human beings who are involved in the sacrament to accomplish his saving intention.

Water is a good symbol for what God does in Baptism because it carries the imagery of cleansing and drowning. Baptism cleanses us from our sin and drowns our old selves. It is not water itself that does these things, but the word of God.

Baptism is not, as some people treat it, an end in itself. It is a once-for-all event, but it is also the beginning of a process. It is the opening chapter of our story of faith. Our faith can grow or decrease; we can experience times of crisis and times of strength. Yet Baptism offers a firm foundation to which our faith can always return.

Baptism emphasizes our personhood. Sometimes people and institutions dehumanize us by treating us only as objects, as means of production, or as numbers. We are more than these. We are persons who have a relationship with God. In Baptism God calls us by name and we become known to him. Baptism makes it clear that our worth depends on God's promises, not on our views of ourselves or the views others have of us.

Baptism unites us to the death and resurrection of Christ. We are baptized into his death so that we might die to sin. We are raised with him into life so that we might walk in newness of life (Rom. 6:3-8).

THE WORD OF THE GOSPEL 243

Baptism brings us communion with Christ, life and a future with God, and unity with other Christians.

Some denominations reject the practice of baptizing small children because they are not old enough to speak for themselves. It is difficult to determine from the New Testament what the earliest Christian practice was in this area. The book of Acts reports the baptism of entire households (16:15, 33), but the earliest explicit mention of infant baptism dates from after 200 A.D. More important than the practice of the early church is whether infant baptism is consistent with the *perspective* of the New Testament. The theology of Paul gives us no reason to object to the practice. Paul considered Baptism to be an act of God that is received as a gift. Moreover, Baptism always presumes the context of the Christian community.

There is no doubt that the practice of infant baptism has sometimes been abused. Too often persons have been baptized without any commitment of parents or sponsors to bring them up within the Christian community. On the other hand, infant baptism is a marvelous sign of the grace of God.

4. Holy Communion

The Christian celebration of Holy Communion was instituted by Christ during his Last Supper with his disciples. Paul gives us the oldest version of Jesus' words at that meal:

The Lord Jesus on the night when he was betrayed took bread, and when he had given thanks, he broke it, and said, "This is my body which is for you. Do this in remembrance of me." In the same way also the cup, after supper, saying, "This cup is the new covenant in my blood. Do this, as often as you drink it, in remembrance of me." For as often as you eat this bread and drink the cup, you proclaim the Lord's death until he comes (1 Cor. 11:23-26; see also Matt. 26:26-29; Mark 14:22-25; Luke 22:17-20).

Jesus' celebration of the Last Supper gives the central focus to Holy Communion. The Christian community is a holy people gathered around the table of the Lord to receive, along with the bread and wine, his own body and blood, signs of our salvation in him. There are also several other important biblical themes that help us understand the meaning of the Lord's Supper.

● *The Passover sacrifice.* In the Passover meal God's people remembered both their escape from slavery in Egypt and their entry into the promised land. A lamb was traditionally eaten as a reminder of the lambs that were sacrificed to save Israel from the plague of death (Exod. 12:21-27). The early Christians understood the strong parallels between the Passover and the Lord's Supper. Like the Passover, the Last Supper was celebrated on the night before God's great act of deliverance for his people. But in this case Jesus himself took the place of the Passover lamb. He gave his life so that God's people might find

freedom. Like Moses, he led his people out of slavery into freedom, through death to life.

● *Meals of fellowship.* The Gospels repeatedly emphasize that Jesus ate with "tax collectors and sinners." By associating with such people Jesus made it clear that he had come "to seek and to save the lost" (Luke 19:10). In the ancient world, those who ate at the same table were considered friends. No one would eat with someone with whom they were having a quarrel. This is why religious people were so upset at Jesus. By eating with sinners he implied that such people could be acceptable in the eyes of God.

Jesus chose the company of sinful human beings. Holy Communion can be understood as a continuation of Jesus' meals of fellowship with sinners and outcasts. By eating with sinners like us, Jesus expresses his love for us and acceptance of us. We can never earn such communion with God, but he graciously gives it to us. At the same time he makes it possible for us to have true communion with each other. He breaks down all barriers of sin, social status, and education and gives us unity. The symbols of that unity are the sharing of one loaf and one cup.

When he instituted Holy Communion, Jesus twice said the words, "Do this for the remembrance of me." The Greek word used for "remembrance" has a much deeper meaning than our English word. When we remember Jesus in the Lord's Supper we are not just calling him to mind. Through our remembrance of him he actually reveals himself to us in the present moment.

Luke reports an appearance by the resurrected Jesus on the road to Emmaus in which two disciples did not recognize who it was who walked with them. But when they sat down to eat, he "took the bread and blessed, and broke it, and gave it to them." At that point, "their eyes were opened and they recognized him" (24:13-35). Like the disciples on their way to Emmaus, Christians see Jesus revealed and present in the "breaking of bread" of Holy Communion.

● *Thanksgiving.* When we celebrate Holy Communion, we give thanks for all that God has done for us. We remember his creation of the world, his saving acts in Israel's history, the messages he gave to his prophets, and especially the gift of his Son Jesus Christ. For this reason Holy Communion is often called the "Eucharist"—the giving of thanks. Jesus said, "Do this for the remembrance of me," and the "this" includes his giving of thanks to God. The Eucharist is a model for all of Christian life, which is a life of thanksgiving. Paul wrote, "be filled with the Spirit. . . . always and for everything giving thanks in the name of our Lord Jesus Christ to God the Father" (Eph. 5:18-20).

● *A feast of the kingdom.* In Luke 14 Jesus compares the kingdom of God to a great banquet. God's servant is sent to tell people, "Come; for all is now ready" (14:17). Many of those who are invited find excuses and decline the gracious invitation. But

God insists on extending the invitation to everyone and anyone who is willing to come as his guest.

The connection between Holy Communion and the future feast of God's kingdom is made even more clear in Luke 22. There Jesus says, "I have earnestly desired to eat this passover with you before I suffer; for I tell you I shall not eat it until it is fulfilled in the kingdom of God" (vv. 15-16). Christians look forward to the time when God will fulfill his kingdom and they can sit down to eat the feast of celebration with their Lord. In the meantime, every celebration of Communion is a foretaste of the feast to come, a means by which we begin to experience God's kingdom here and now.

Summary

● Announcing the gospel of God's forgiveness and forgiving the sins of others are part of the ministry that belongs to every Christian.

● Pastors have the specific tasks of preaching and teaching the word of God to the church and presiding over the celebration of the sacraments.

● The liturgy is an action of the entire worshiping community that can embrace and sustain us.

● The task of preaching is to make Jesus Christ known: his coming, life, suffering, death, resurrection, and his will for us today.

● Baptism brings adoption into the family of God,

the forgiveness of sins, granting of the Holy Spirit, and incorporation into the church.

● The Christian community is a holy people gathered around the table of the Lord to receive, along with the bread and wine, his own body and blood, signs of our salvation in him.

For reflection

But how are men to call upon him in whom they have not believed? And how are they to believe in him of whom they have never heard? And how are they to hear without a preacher? And how can men preach unless they are sent? As it is written, "How beautiful are the feet of those who preach good news!" . . . So faith comes from what is heard, and what is heard comes by the preaching of Christ.

Rom. 10:14-15, 17

You are the bread of life,
O, Lord, to me.
Your holy Word the truth
That rescues me.
Give me to eat and live
With you above;
Teach me to love your truth,
For you are love.

Oh, send your Spirit, Lord,
Now unto me,
That he may touch my eyes
And make me see.
Show me the truth concealed
Within your Word,
And in your book revealed
I see my Lord.

   Mary A. Lathbury (1841-1913)
   Lutheran Book of Worship 235

As each member of the congregation listens to the
absolution in church and says his "Amen," he is just
as much at the pronouncing end in relationship to his
fellow members as he is at the receiving end in relation to God.

   John A. T. Robinson
   On Being the Church in the World
   (Westminster, 1960), p. 81

At the end of the prayers we embrace each other
with a kiss. The bread is brought to the president of
the brethren, and a cup of water and wine: this he
takes, and offers praise and glory to the Father of all,
through the name of his Son and of the Holy Spirit;
and he gives thanks at length for our being granted

these gifts at his hand. When he has finished the prayers and the thanksgiving all the people present give their assent with *Amen,* a Hebrew word signifying "So be it." When the president has given thanks and all the people have assented, those whom we call "deacons" give a portion of the bread over which thanksgiving has been offered, and of the wine and water, to each of those who are present; and they carry them away to those who are absent.

Justin Martyr (c. 100-165)
The Early Christian Fathers
(Oxford, 1956), p. 85

To put it most simply, the power, effect, benefit, fruit, and purpose of Baptism is to save. No one is baptized in order to become a prince, but as the words say, to "be saved." To be saved, we know, is nothing else than to be delivered from sin, death, and the devil and to enter into the kingdom of Christ and live with him forever.

Martin Luther (1483-1546)
Large Catechism, *Book of Concord*
(Fortress, 1959), p. 439

Almighty God,
grant that we,

who have been redeemed
from the old life of sin
by our baptism
into the death and resurrection
of your Son Jesus Christ,
may be renewed
in your Holy Spirit
to live in righteousness
and true holiness;
through Jesus Christ our Lord.
Amen.

Lutheran Book of Worship
Prayer 200, p. 47

16

The Mission
of the Church

The early Christians could not keep quiet about what God had done in Jesus Christ. "Out of the abundance of the heart the mouth speaks" (Matt. 12:34). From the very beginning, the church has responded to God's love by becoming a vehicle for Christ's mission in the world. The Holy Spirit has created the church, and the church exists for the sake of the world. It is a communion of saints that cannot keep its faith, its love, and its gifts to itself.

Mission is not something added to the Christian faith. The message of what God has done in Jesus Christ is meant for all persons in all times and places. Mission is not just one of the church's many activities. In Acts 1:8 Jesus places it beyond the mere fulfilling of an obligation: "You shall receive power when the Holy Spirit has come upon you; and you shall be my witnesses . . . to the end of the earth." Through the power of the Holy Spirit the church not only engages in mission, it *is* mission.

1. The nature of the church's mission

God uses sinful, error-prone human beings to extend the message of salvation to all people. In spite of our unfaithfulness, God remains faithful. The people of God have been given many gifts and places to use them. The mission of the church involves every believer. That mission takes place wherever people are in need of help, encouragement, love, and forgiveness.

The mission of the church includes two closely related tasks, *evangelism* and *service*. Evangelism simply means making the gospel known. Service means caring for the needs of people. These two tasks must not be completely separated from each other.

The close relationship between evangelism and service is illustrated by the story in Acts 6 of the appointment of seven deacons in the Jerusalem church. The apostles needed their help because they wanted to devote more time to preaching and teaching. The deacons were to oversee the daily distribution of food to the widows in the community. Yet before long the deacons, too, were involved in preaching the gospel (vv. 8-10). The New Testament makes it very clear that genuine love for God will express itself in love for one's neighbor:

If any one says, "I love God," and hates his brother, he is a liar; for he who does not love his brother whom he has seen, cannot love God whom he has not seen" (1 John 4:20; see also Luke 22:27; John 13:1-15; James 2:15-16).

Among the first Christians, love for God and love for one's neighbor were interconnected. They still are.

2. The task of evangelism

The New Testament states that God "desires all men to be saved and to come to the knowledge of the truth" (1 Tim. 2:4). Evangelism is the task of making this truth—Jesus Christ—known to all people. By making the good news of God's grace known, Christians tell what God has done for human beings, reject all false gods and idols, and point to the future God is creating.

The task of evangelism goes far beyond the public preaching and teaching of the gospel. Every Christian has something to share about the love of God and the gifts of God. Every person has unique capabilities that enable him or her to touch the life of another. Every believer has some kind of ministry. The gospel can be communicated in as many different forms as there are varieties of human experience, and each person has a unique way of bearing witness to it. Through it all, the same Lord Jesus Christ is proclaimed.

The great challenge of evangelism is for Christians to become open to the people all around them. God has called us to minister to those we know in our families, work, and outside interests. We need to listen to their hurts and joys and look for ways to make God's love known through our own words and actions. When we are sensitive to their real needs and allow ourselves to reflect the gospel, the Holy Spirit will bring the fruit.

The question has often been raised about what will happen to those who die before having an opportunity to hear the gospel. The Bible does not give a clear answer to this question. We know it is God's will that all should be saved, but God has not revealed everything to us. We must trust in his grace. At the same time, however, we sense the urgency of the church's evangelical task. It is our responsibility to *tell* people about the good news of Christ and to let that good news take shape in our lives.

3. The task of service

In its original sense, the New Testament Greek word for service *(diakonia)* meant serving at tables (see Luke 17:8). But in the early church, "service" took on the broader meaning of attending to the needs of others in the name of Jesus (Mark 10:42-45; 1 Peter 4:8-11). Jesus said,

You call me Teacher and Lord; and you are right, for so I am. If I then, your Lord and Teacher, have washed your feet, you also ought to wash one another's feet. For I have given you an example, that you also should do as I have done to you. Truly, truly, I say to you, a servant is not greater than his master; nor is he who is sent greater than he who sent him (John 13:13-16).

Christians have been given an example of service by

the Lord himself. The people of God carry out this task in every aspect of life. The world is full of persons who are in need: the poor, the hungry, refugees, prisoners, the unemployed, the chemically dependent, victims of violence and repression, the lonely. Some of these needs are as stark and clear as the faces on the television news. Others draw little attention, and many suffer alone.

Christians address the needs of the world on many different levels and in many different ways. Some things can be done immediately within one's own realm of experience. Other needs require concerted effort by many people working together as advocates for large-scale change. At all levels and in many different ways, service is needed.

Family life

Christians concern themselves with their own relationships with parents, children, brothers, and sisters. The family is a primary setting in which the love of God can be expressed. Many problems related to family life need the attention of church and society, such as disrespect for life, irresponsible sexual behavior, child abuse, marriage problems, and orphaned or abandoned children.

Societal life

Our life with others in society provides ample opportunities to become involved in improving structures and relationships. Some primary concerns are

ministry to the lonely, the imprisoned, the mentally
ill, the chemically dependent, awareness and response
to the needs of the handicapped, improved medical
care, refugee resettlement, education, and support for
victims of violence, abuse, and exploitation.

Economic life

God has given gifts in creation to be used for the
benefit of all people. Christians strive for improved
ethics in business, equal opportunity for all persons, a
more just distribution of resources, assistance for those
in acute need, and elimination of structures that per-
petuate poverty.

Government

In public life Christians press for government respect for basic human rights, for increased honesty
and responsibility among those who hold public office,
for laws that protect the helpless and restrain the powerful, and for prison reform.

World

On a world scale, Christians join together in advo-
cacy for those things that better express God's will for
creation and for all people, including protection of the
environment, economic development, a just distribution of food and other resources, disaster relief, the
search for sources of energy that are safe and abundant, and for a true peace based on respect and justice
among all nations.

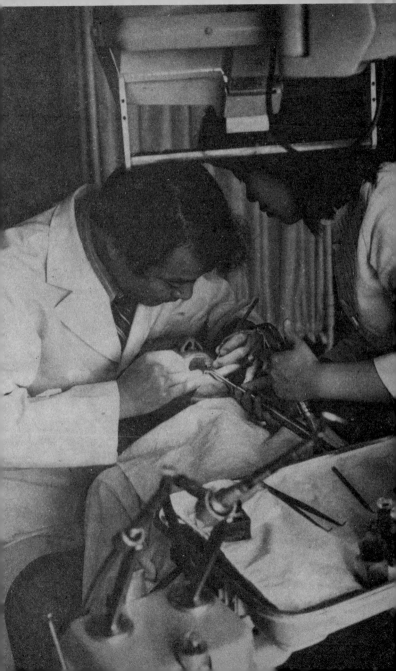

Service to the world is not an option for Christians. It is an essential part of being Jesus' disciples. The parables about the final judgment and the good Samaritan strongly reinforce this theme (Matt. 25:31-45; Luke 10:25-37). Those who have received the love of God in Jesus Christ cannot keep it to themselves. They share it with others as their faith becomes active in love (Gal. 5:6).

Summary

● The mission of the church involves every believer, and includes both evangelism and service.

● Love for God and love for one's neighbor are always closely connected.

● Evangelism is the task of making Jesus Christ known to all people.

● Every Christian has something to share about the love of God and the gifts of God.

● Christians have been given an example of service by the Lord himself.

● Christians address the needs of the world on many different levels and in many different ways.

For reflection

Is not this the fast that I choose:
to loose the bonds of wickedness,
to undo the thongs of the yoke,
to let the oppressed go free,

and to break every yoke?
Is it not to share your bread
with the hungry,
and bring the homeless poor
into your house;
when you see the naked,
to cover him,
and not to hide yourself
from your own flesh? . . .
Then you shall call,
and the Lord will answer;
you shall cry, and he will say,
Here I am.

Isa. 58:6-7, 9

The wedge that has been driven between evangelistic and evangelical is most unfortunate. Even "evangelical" is understood by some as applying only to certain conservative Christians. Any Christian who is not "evangelical" in the sense that he owes his life to the gospel is a strange and questionable Christian indeed. Any Christian theology that is not evangelistic in the sense that it fails to share the gifts given by God is a strange and questionable "Christian theology."

Ralph W. Quere
Evangelical Witness
(Augsburg, 1975), p. 11

Christian service goes beyond alleviation of ills to the eradication of conditions that create ills and the planting of the kingdom of God on earth. Christian service is not limited only to catastrophic needs. It is an ongoing program to bring blessing to all people all the time in all places.

Rolf A. Syrdal
Go, Make Disciples
(Augsburg, 1977), p. 104

The church, as the community of the saved ones, has been thought of as the gathering of those who have "their ticket to heaven." We tend to forget . . . that salvation is not so much a prize won as a responsibility given. Without its "for what?" salvation is meaningless.

Orlando E. Costas
The Church and Its Mission
(Tyndale, 1974), p. 249

There is a distinction between the mission of God in Jesus Christ and the mission of the church, in the sense that the church cannot be the atoner, the revivifier, and the restorer of mankind to God. The church cannot assume the mission of being lord and savior of mankind. Jesus commissions his people to mission not to repeat, let alone replace, what he has done, but to witness to it, to testify to its reality in him, to proclaim that he is the reconciler and lord of the world. The mission of the church is specifically defined: to be a witness to Jesus Christ (Acts 1:8).

Emerito P. Nacpil
What Asian Christians Are Thinking
(New Day, 1976), p. 282

O Spirit of the living God,
In all the fullness of your grace,
Wherever human feet have trod,
Descend on our apostate race.

Give tongues of fire and hearts of love
To preach the reconciling Word;
Give pow'r and unction from above,
Where'er this blessed sound is heard.

James Montgomery (1771-1854)
Lutheran Book of Worship 388

Part Six

How Should We Live?

It does not fit today's popular mood, but we all need fidelity: the intention to do what we say, to accept discipline in order to solidify the good. Fidelity means more than not sleeping around the neighborhood. It means that we have made a promise, a commitment, and that we have accepted the limitations that are part of that promise. There are great satisfactions in saying, "I have done what I undertook to do."

Joseph Sittler
The Christian Century
September 26, 1979, p. 916

17

Love and Commitment

A study of Christian teachings would be incomplete if it did not take into account the consequences of faith for life. The gospel of Jesus Christ puts all of life in a new light. Christians have been freed from the power of sin and the burden of the past to be living expressions of God's will in the world.

After explaining the significance of the gospel to the Christians at Rome, Paul wrote:

I appeal to you therefore, brethren, by the mercies of God, to present your bodies as a living sacrifice, holy and acceptable to God, which is your spiritual worship. Do not be conformed to this world but be transformed by the renewal of your mind, that you may prove what is the will of God, what is good and acceptable and perfect (Rom. 12:1-2).

Paul understood Christian life to be an all-encompassing process of transformation. Nothing is excluded from the lordship of Christ. All issues, roles, and values are examined from the perspective of the gospel, to discover that which is "good and acceptable and perfect."

1. What is God's intention for life?

During the course of his earthly ministry, Jesus often spoke of the will of God. He was frequently questioned about his interpretation of various passages of the Old Testament law, and his replies astounded those who understood God's will only in terms of legal or ritual requirements. The Gospels report that he was once asked to summarize the law by naming the greatest commandment:

But when the Pharisees heard that he had silenced the Sadducees, they came together. And one of them, a lawyer, asked him a question, to test him. "Teacher, which is the great commandment in the law?" And he said to him, "You shall love the Lord your God with all your heart, and with all your soul, and with all your mind. This is the great and first commandment. And a second is like it, You shall love your neighbor as yourself. On these two commandments depend all the law and the prophets" (Matt. 22:34-40; see also Mark 12:28-34).

Jesus understood the basic intention of God for our lives in terms of love. God wills that our love for him be complete and undivided, and that we love our neighbors to the same degree that we would love ourselves. Luke's gospel reports that Jesus was questioned further about love for one's neighbor:

But he, desiring to justify himself, said to Jesus, "And who is my neighbor?" Jesus replied, "A man was going down from Jerusalem to Jericho, and he fell among robbers, who stripped him and beat him, and departed, leaving him half dead. Now by chance a priest was going down that road; and when he saw him he passed by on the other side. So likewise a Levite, when he came to the place and saw him, passed by on the other side. But a Samaritan, as he journeyed, came to where he was; and when he saw him, he had compassion, and went to him and bound up his wounds, pouring on oil and wine; then he set him on his own beast and brought him to an inn, and took care of him. And the next day he took out two denarii and gave them to the innkeeper, saying, 'Take care of him; and whatever more you spend, I will repay you when I come back.' Which of these three, do you think, proved neighbor to the man who fell among the robbers?" He said, "The one who showed mercy on him." And Jesus said to him, "Go and do likewise" (Luke 10:29-37).

The parable of the good Samaritan shows that love for one's neighbor means much more than being willing to help the people who live next door. The Samaritan went out of his way and experienced great inconvenience to help the man on the side of the road. Further, the two men were of very different backgrounds. The Samaritans were despised by the Jews, and the two groups had few dealings with each other. The Samaritan had to overcome ethnic and emotional barriers to help the traveler from Jerusalem.

Love for one's neighbor, then, goes far beyond feelings for those who are familiar to us. Love reaches out and overcomes the things that separate persons from each other. In fact, Jesus commands us to love even our enemies:

You have heard that it was said, "You shall love your neighbor and hate your enemy." But I say to you, Love your enemies and pray for those who persecute you, so that you may be sons of your Father who is in heaven; for he makes his sun rise on the evil and on the good, and sends rain on the just and on the unjust. For if you love those who love you, what reward have you? Do not even the tax collectors do the same? And if you salute only your brethren, what more are you doing than others? Do not even the Gentiles do the same? You, therefore, must be perfect, as your heavenly Father is perfect (Matt. 5:43-48).

The will of God for human beings can be understood in terms of love that is genuine, complete, and specific. It is not possible to love God and at the same time hate our neighbors (1 John 4:20-21). Those who love God prove themselves neighbors to others.

Love is a gift. Christians can love because God has first loved them (1 John 4:19). As Father, Son, and Holy Spirit, God creates, redeems, and lives in them. God has given believers many gifts, especially faith, hope, and love. Of these three, love is the greatest (1 Cor. 13:13):

If I speak in the tongues of men and of angels, but have not love, I am a noisy gong or a clanging cymbal. And if I have prophetic powers, and understand all mysteries and

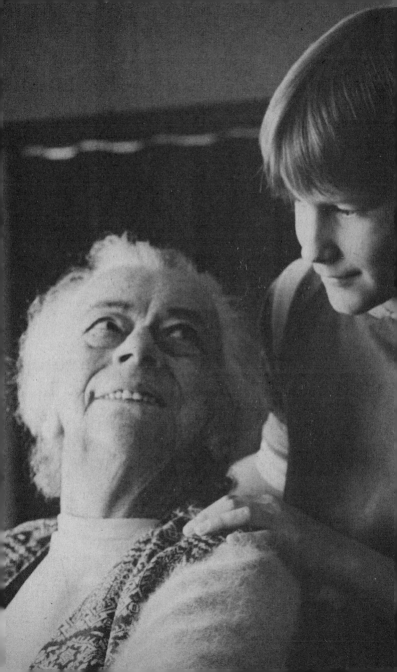

all knowledge, and if I have all faith, so as to remove mountains, but have not love, I am nothing. If I give away all I have, and if I deliver my body to be burned, but have not love, I gain nothing (1 Cor. 13:1-3).

2. What are the dimensions of love?

Love is one of the most used—and abused—words in the English language. It is sung about, thought about, agonized about. But what is it? *Webster's Dictionary* gives a whole range of meanings for the word: attraction, desire, or affection; warm attachment, enthusiasm, or devotion; or the attraction based on sexual desire. Love takes many forms and is expressed in many ways.

One way to distinguish the various dimensions of love is to look at the principal words for "love" in the Greek New Testament: *eros, philia,* and *agape.* Although their meanings overlap to some degree, these words also have distinctly different connotations.

● *Eros* refers to a natural human feeling related to beauty, virtue, or goodness. It includes but is not limited to sexuality. Because it includes a striving for personal fulfillment, it has an egocentric quality.

● *Philia* implies a social quality of love that expresses feelings for friends and neighbors as well as for family. It includes kindness, courtesy, and concern for the welfare of all people.

● *Agape* refers to love that is selfless and undeserved. God's love is *agape* because it cannot be earned, but only received as a gift and passed on to others.

Agape expresses itself through *philia* and *eros,* moving them beyond self-centeredness. It prevents *eros* from being distorted by human sinfulness and makes it responsible and personal. It keeps *philia* from limiting itself to friends and equals, opening persons to love even their enemies. *Agape* is the love that ties all other love to its source in God.

According to the Bible, love is more than a feeling. It is a power that initiates and sustains relationships. Love takes responsibility for others and is expressed through commitment to their welfare. Love binds people together and keeps people together in spite of the effects of sin, weakness, and human failings. Love can do these things because it is rooted in God, who remains faithful in his commitment to us.

3. How does God's love express itself?

The model for human love is the love of God revealed in the Old and New Testaments. As God has loved us, so we are to love one another (John 15:12-13). To be able to love another person presupposes that we ourselves have experienced love. God has committed himself to us in the gospel, and because of his commitment we are able to commit ourselves to each other.

God loves us and shows himself to be committed to

our welfare in several ways. Each way serves as a model for what our love also is intended to be:

● God's love is *undeserved*. Everything God has given us is a gift. We were created in love and given the gift of life. We were chosen to be saved through Jesus Christ apart from any merit of our own. In fact, it was while we were still sinners that Christ died for us (Rom. 5:6-8). The Holy Spirit who lives in us is a continuing reminder of God's grace to us. Because God loves us, he has committed himself to us even though we do not deserve his gifts.

● God's love is *steadfast*. One of the Old Testament's common words for the love of God is *hesed*, or "steadfast love." The refrain of Psalm 136 is a striking reminder of God's faithfulness to his people (see RSV). Even though we have taken God's love and grace for granted and sinned against him, he has remained faithful to us. He never stops pursuing us.

● God's love is *forgiving*. Our human love is often clouded by the sense of having been offended by another. We easily hold grudges and remind each other of past mistakes. God does not treat us in this fashion, but rather wants an open and honest relationship with us and desires to forgive our sins. A willingness to forgive is also to be a mark of our relationships with each other (Matt. 18:23-35).

● God's love is *reconciling*. Forgiveness is closely related to wholeness between persons. In Jesus Christ God has broken down the barriers between sinful

human beings and himself (Col. 1:15-23). God desires that we be reconciled with him and also with one another.

● God's love is *renewing*. God has made a new beginning in Christ, and through him he will make all things new (Rev. 21:5). God's love never becomes old and worn out, but always seeks new expression. He loves even the dead into life again, and makes it possible for us to experience a sense of newness with each other.

The Christian life is full of challenges. The effects of sin linger on in the world, even though God has defeated its power. Yet the love of God supports and undergirds us. Even though we are often faithless, we can pursue the calling God has given us in the world, knowing that he is faithful. Christ has called us to a life of discipleship marked by love. He will not desert us as we follow where he leads.

Summary

● Jesus understood the basic intention of God for our lives in terms of love.

● Jesus commands us to love even our enemies.

● Christians can love because God has first loved them.

● Love has many dimensions and is expressed in many ways.

● Love is rooted in God, who remains faithful in his commitment to us.

● We can pursue the calling God has given us in the world, knowing that he is faithful.

For reflection

Love is patient and kind; love is not jealous or boastful; it is not arrogant or rude. Love does not insist on its own way; it is not irritable or resentful; it does not rejoice at wrong, but rejoices in the right. Love bears all things, believes all things, hopes all things, endures all things. Love never ends. . . .

1 Cor. 13:4-8

Love as an emotion cannot be commanded. Either love is something other than emotion or the Great Commandment is meaningless.

Paul Tillich (1886-1965)
Love, Power and Justice
(Oxford, 1954), p. 4

When we think of love we tend to think of spectacular emotions and heroic acts for the beloved. But little of life is passed in moments of intensity, important as they are. The best relationships are built up, like a fine lacquer finish, with the accumulated layers of many acts of kindness.

Alan Loy McGinnis
The Friendship Factor
(Augsburg, 1979), p. 51

Faith has to do with the basis, the ground on which we stand. Hope is reaching out for something to come. Love is just being there and acting.

Emil Brunner
Faith, Hope and Love
(Westminster, 1956), p. 61

The expression of God's will and purpose, his love and compassion, are manifest in Jesus Christ not just through his consciousness but through his decisions and acts, through obedience even unto death, through acts of mercy and healing bringing wholeness not to humanity in the abstract but to men and women in their concrete personal existence, anxious, guilty and mortal, living, struggling and dying, seeking, doubting and finding, hoping for the kingdom to come but not yet knowing that in Jesus Christ it has already come.

S. J. Samartha
What Asian Christians Are Thinking
(New Day, 1976), p. 224

O God, my faithful God,
True fountain ever flowing,
Without whom nothing is,
All perfect gifts bestowing. . . .

Help me, as you have taught,
To love both great and small,
And, by your Spirit's might,
To live at peace with all.

    Johann Heermann (1585-1647)
    Lutheran Book of Worship 504

18

Sexuality and Marriage

In recent years there has been a great upheaval in the traditional views of sexuality and marriage. Society has undergone what some call a "sexual revolution." Many people are questioning the concept of a lifelong monogamous marriage. They claim that it doesn't work and hampers sexual fulfillment. If Christians are to make responsible contributions to current discussions of issues related to marriage and sexuality, they cannot be content just to repeat traditional rules. They will make use of the insights of Scripture and also of scientific study as they seek to give faithful expression to God's intentions.

1. What can science tell us about sexuality and sexual behavior?

Within the span of just one century, sex has gone from a forbidden subject to a public fascination. Scientific research on the subject of human sexual response has learned a great deal, and a wide variety of books and manuals analyze every aspect of the biology of sex.

While our understanding of sexual development, response, and technique has greatly increased, science has not provided us with a clear perspective on the proper context and standards for human sexual behavior. Some social scientists say all sexual practices are permissible and desirable so long as they occur between consenting adults. Others insist that sexual fulfillment comes only through long-term relationships of love and trust.

The confusion among social scientists over the ethics of sex is disturbing, but should not be surprising. The methods of science are intended to help us describe reality. They enable us to say what *is*, not what *should be*. Scientists who tell us what correct sexual conduct is are not speaking as scientists. They are expressing their opinions on ethics. Their views may be right or wrong, but science by itself cannot prove or disprove what they say.

The basic difference between science and ethics is at the root of the present controversy over sex education in the public schools. Society attempts to communicate factual information about sexuality to young people through the school system, yet biology does not provide a complete context for the role and meaning of sexuality in human life. Some school systems have tried to resolve this problem by providing social and psychological information together with biological instruction. Yet so long as society as a whole cannot agree on what right sexual behavior is, its attempts at a complete and balanced approach to sex education will encounter difficulty. Sex education in the public schools may well supplement the ethical training provided by parents and the church, but it cannot replace such training.

2. How should we understand sexuality and sexual behavior?

Human sexuality includes all that we are as human beings. It is related to everything we feel, think, say, and do. Sexuality at the very least is biological, psychological, cultural, social, and spiritual. It is as much of the mind as of the body, of the community as of the individual. To be a person is to be a sexual being. Physically and spiritually we have a deep desire to seek another person with whom we can feel one.

The Old Testament expresses the human search for partners in the imagery of Genesis 2. God caused Adam to fall into a deep sleep, taking a rib from his side, made a woman, and brought her to him. So Adam found a fitting mate (v. 23). Adam's words express the age-old astonishment of persons who unexpectedly rediscover themselves in their relationship with someone of the opposite sex.

God has created all that is, seen and unseen. God created human life, male and female (Gen. 1:27-31; Matt. 19:4-5). Each person is a unique creation of God. Each of us has a special identity; each receives

individual abilities and opportunities to use them; each is called to use the gift of life in service to God, to our neighbors, and to ourselves. Sexual human life is a gracious gift, a sacred trust, from God.

There is a growing emphasis on the need for equality between women and men. Equality does not mean uniformity, for each person is unique and there are general differences between the sexes that go beyond physical traits. Yet it is no longer possible to speak of "typical" female or male behavior or tendencies. Fulfillment lies not in the achievement of sameness, but in the full development of the capacities given to each.

The human capacity to participate in sexual behavior is God's design for continuing the human race. Sexual behavior can also fulfill the divine design for enhancing the joy and renewing the vows of love and marriage. It can be a means for knowing ourselves and growing as persons. Based on mutual trust and commitment it can be a person-to-person exercise of honor and dignity, of respect for our self and for the other person, of forgiveness and acceptance of one another's imperfections.

Sexual expression is *not* in and of itself evil, lustful, a duty to be done or a burden to be borne. It is unfortunate that Christians so often have taught such views. Yet sexual intercourse or sexual satisfaction is not the highest or noblest goal in human life. The God-given sacredness and joy of sexual expression must be placed in the context of the total range of a person's relationships. Sexual expression must also be

viewed in the perspective of growth, wholeness, fulfillment, striving to accomplish in families and communities the best that life under God can offer.

One need not engage in sexual intercourse either
to survive physically or to enjoy physical and mental
health. Sex drives are very powerful, and intercourse
is essential for the continuation of the human race,
but human beings are not the slaves of their sexual instincts. We can consciously control our behavior. Sex
is a gift of God, but celibacy is neither abnormal nor
a denial of personhood.

All persons need opportunities to relate wholesome-
ly with persons both of their own and of the other
sex. Human beings are created for fellowship, for
sociability, for caring, and for the sharing of fears,
hopes, and dreams. All persons, single or married,
need avenues for the exchange of affectional, friendly,
self-giving love. Such wholesome exchanges of caring
between and among persons are an integral part of
that community known as the body of Christ.

The Scriptures extol the joys of sexual relationships.
Adam expressed joy over Eve. It is significant that the
Hebrew word meaning "to know" is used both for the
relationship between God and a human being and for
the sexual union of men and women: "Adam knew Eve
his wife" (Gen. 4:1). The Song of Solomon is a sensi-
tively erotic poem of joy over the sexual expressions
of love between a man and a woman. 1 Corinthians 7
frankly addresses the desirability of sexual expression
between husband and wife. A number of the Psalms,

notably 127 and 128, sing the blessings of a happy marriage. Yet the Scriptures, particularly Proverbs and the Prophets, also recognize the bitterness and pain of sexual behavior that alienates the sexes from each other and from God.

Sexual behavior that violates human dignity and integrity is sinful. The Scriptures identify such behavior with acts of rape, violence, incest, seduction, adultery, prostitution, and some forms of homosexual behavior, to name the more obvious. These bring individual hurt or harm and alienation from God and from one's neighbors.

There are people who are ready to exploit the evil uses of sex to increase their own power or profit. Major industries are built up around satisfying "the lust of the flesh and the lust of the eyes and the pride of life" (1 John 2:16). Among the many forms of exploitive sexual behavior are those that:

- exploit children and youth, men and women, as in pornography and prostitution;
- take advantage of persons who are ill, helpless, dependent, handicapped, or of little power;
- endanger, cause physical or emotional injury, or do long-term harm;
- use threat, force, or prestige to persuade an otherwise unwilling person to engage in sexual behavior;
- engage promiscuously in a public quest for new sexual partners;

● break promises and violate commitments that people have made in the responsible exercise of their free will;

● build trade and commerce based on satisfying prurient interest;

● violate standards of public decency;

● invade the privacy and self-respect of others;

● magnify sexuality and sexual behavior in print, on the screen, and on the stage in ways irrelevant to the product or incidental to the dominant theme.

The Bible understands God's intentions for sexual relationships between women and men to include trust, commitment, self-giving, sacrifice, and forgiveness. Sexual fulfillment comes through love, and love includes responsibility for others, respect, compassion, and reliability. Separated from love, sex degrades human beings by remaining only on the level of physical gratification. This is why the Bible speaks so highly of marriage and so negatively of sexual relationships that are violent, self-serving, or casual.

Sexual intimacy requires the security that marriage provides. When sexual intercourse is not expressed within the binding lifelong relationship of marriage, the result may be a series of trial relationships in which individuals use each other to satisfy their own desires. When intercourse is isolated from an enduring personal relationship, intimacy often leads to hurt and disillusionment.

The art of waiting for an appropriate complete ex-

pression of one's sexuality separates love from self-gratification. Finding a partner with whom one can share a permanent sexual relationship requires patience, self-control, and consideration—the same qualities that are essential to a good marriage.

3. How should we understand marriage?

Marriage is a structure of human life built into the creation by the Creator, who made us male and female. Sexual differences are of God's good design, intended to bring joy and enrichment to human life as well as to provide for procreation. The essence of marriage is that two persons become "one flesh" in every aspect of their relationship (Gen. 2:24).

Marriage is a means by which God places us into an intimate relationship with another, signifying that we were not meant to be alone. It is a relationship between a woman and a man that undergirds their love and gives shape to their life together. Marriage ceremonies serve as symbols of public acceptance of the responsibility of husbands and wives to each other.

A marriage exists when a man and a woman agree to live out their lives together and their decision is publicly confirmed. After a legal ceremony, the two persons are no longer connected merely by affection, but also by legally binding vows. These provide their union with a sense of security, protect any children they may have, and reinforce the commitment of each one to the marriage. To these vows and the force of law the Christian community adds, in its celebrations of marriage, the blessing of God, the prayers of Christians, and the promises of family, friends, and the church to support the relationship.

Christian people seek the fulfillment of their marriage in Christ as they grow in loving one another even as Christ has loved them, as they learn to forgive one another in the spirit of Christ, and as they draw on the resources that the Lord of the church makes available to his people. Marriage involves both interdependence and reciprocity. God intends that persons should enter marriage expectantly, awaiting the gifts of the other person. By sharing with each other, married persons find security and happiness. If there is complete dependence on one of the persons and the other partner does not contribute to the marriage, the result can be disaster. Marriage should be a relationship of mutuality through which both partners grow.

Marriage is not a structure in which all Christians should be expected to exercise their calling. For some, singleness may be the best way they can serve God and their neighbors. Whether we are married or single, our faith in God frees us from the need to conform to the pressures of society. Either way, we live our lives in service to him.

When we prepare to decide on a particular person as a life-partner, we need to know not only that person, but also ourselves. We must come to terms with our own interests, needs, gifts, and weaknesses. We must ask whether the two of us will be willing to

give of ourselves and work out our differences. We need to ask whether both of us can turn to God and ask for his help and guidance in times of difficulty. Submission of our individual wills to Christ makes it easier for us to help, respect, and love each other (Eph. 5:21).

The unity God intends for marriage requires a life-long commitment of husband and wife to each other. Love can flourish only in a relationship of faithfulness. A commitment to one another provides the foundation for real freedom and growth. Just as love, faithfulness, and service mark the relationship of Christ and the church, so also they should characterize the relationship of wives and husbands.

The strength and unity of marriage come from mutual recognition and sharing of each other's needs and gifts. This unity recognizes the freedom of husbands and wives to express their own interests as well as their duty to share in those relationships where sharing is essential to the success of the marriage. The unique gifts of wives and husbands should be used, within the harmony of marriage, toward the meaningful goals and purposes of human life assigned by God.

Marriage provides a secure place for a trusting and intimate relationship. It is a way for persons to express the same kind of love with which God loves us. That sort of love is mature, kind, considerate, self-giving, dedicated to the well-being and fulfillment of the other, and faithful to death. It seeks to give rather than to get. This kind of love is the goal and gift of marriage, the quality in which marriage partners ought to grow and mature.

Sexual intercourse expresses the unique union between a husband and wife. By its very nature sexual intercourse expresses a complete commitment to another person. Intercourse should be an expression of love, but love is both richer and more inclusive than the sex act. Sexual harmony is not so much the goal of marriage as a reflection of the total unity and love of the married pair. Sex has often been exploited as an instrument of power and aggression, or falsely portrayed as a panacea, leading many couples to be disappointed with sex as they experience it.

Sometimes sexual intimacy is hindered in spite of the best intentions. There may be a conflict in the relationship that prevents complete openness, or there may be the pressures of time or the obstacle of illness. In such situations, it is important to speak openly of the difficulties involved, bear with each other, and make an extra attempt to meet each other's true needs.

Married Christians seek to fulfill God's intentions, yet all marriages fall short of the ideal. Therefore husbands and wives daily need God's forgiveness for their sins of omission and commission, followed by a readiness to forgive each other. In gratitude toward God they need daily to rededicate themselves to God and to one another, realizing that their marital unity is never completed but always in the process of becoming.

Marriage partners bring with them habits and values acquired from their background and families. Since a marriage involves sharing values, tasks, and responsibilities, couples need to be open about their differences and try to deal with them in constructive ways. Marriage can involve pain and suffering, yet far greater is the pain that comes from a broken relationship between two people who trusted each other. It is in the very experience of meeting crises together that a woman and a man can grow inwardly and discover deeper levels of happiness.

4. How should we understand divorce?

Problems are normal to marriage. Problems and conflicts can be used constructively to further communication and understanding, or they may become destructive of the relationship of love between a husband and wife. When people become involved in marital difficulties, it should be a concern of pastors, relatives, and friends to provide help and understanding in overcoming the conflicts, thereby strengthening and preserving the marriage.

Marriage is by its very nature a lifetime endeavor. The total costs of disruption of a marriage are high, not only for the persons married but also for their children and many others involved. Broken marriages are destructive of family, congregational, and community strength. Therefore couples having difficulties

should be helped to find competent counsel before the marriage itself is threatened.

Divorce is never God's intention. The breakdown of a marriage relationship is the consequence of human sinfulness, leading to a process of alienation from which there seems to be no other way out. Divorce needs to be seen realistically as the breaking of a relationship established by God; the public and legal recognition of an already broken marriage; and the culmination of a process of alienation.

Divorce, according to Jesus, is a concession to the fact and reality of sin in a fallen world. Being the friend of sinners, Jesus did not condemn or drive away divorced persons. Neither did he excuse divorce. Rather, he declared, "What therefore God has joined together, let not man put asunder" (Mark 10:9). He spoke no word by which a man or a woman might rationalize divorce into a righteous act. Jesus did, however, explain divorce as resulting from the hardness of human hearts (Matt. 19:8; Mark 10:5). Divorce arises from self-centeredness or other obstacles a couple cannot or will not overcome.

Those contemplating divorce do so with a sense of the seriousness of their decision, and often with a sense of anguish. Christian spouses will do everything in their power to restore their marriage. Certainly before they decide on divorce they will give themselves time and opportunity to evaluate the total costs of the possible termination of their marriage, for

themselves as well as for their families and others involved.

If, after careful consideration, the marriage relationship is determined to be beyond repair, and the
effects of continuing the marriage are seen to be more
destructive of the welfare of persons than divorce, the
decision for divorce may be recognized as a responsible choice, the lesser of several evils in a fallen
world. Recognizing that each party generally bears
some responsibility for the failure of the marriage, a
decision for divorce may be made in reliance on God's
grace.

The church is called to deal with the problems of
divorce and divorced persons in a loving way rather
than a legalistic way. Christians need to show love
and Christ's spirit of forgiveness toward divorced
persons. These persons should not be the victims of
gossip, ostracism, or undue attention. They need, perhaps more than ever, the bonds of friendship and
communion with the rest of God's people. They continue to be baptized members of Christ's church,
members of his body who gather in his name.

Summary

- Science has informed us about sexual development, response, and technique, but it cannot provide
us with a sexual ethic.

- Human sexuality is a gift of God that must be

placed in the context of the total range of a person's relationships.

● Sexual behavior that violates human dignity and integrity is sinful.

● Marriage is a means by which God places us into an intimate relationship with another, signifying that we were not meant to be alone.

● The unity of marriage requires a lifelong commitment of husband and wife to each other.

● The church is called to deal with the problems of divorce and divorced persons in a loving way rather than a legalistic way.

For reflection

And Jesus called them to him and said to them, "You know that those who are supposed to rule over the Gentiles lord it over them, and their great men exercise authority over them. But it shall not be so among you; but whoever would be great among you must be your servant, and whoever would be first among you must be slave of all. For the Son of man also came not to be served but to serve, and to give his life as a ransom for many."

Mark 10:42-44

Hear us now, our God and Father,
Send your Spirit from above

On this Christian man and woman
Who here make their vows of love!
Bind their hearts in true devotion
Endless as the seashore's sands,
Boundless as the deepest ocean,
Blest and sealed by your own hands.

Give them joy to lighten sorrow!
Give them hope to brighten life!
Go with them to face the morrow,
Stay with them in ev'ry strife.
As your Word has promised, ever
Fill them with your strength and grace,
So that each may serve the other
Till they see you face to face.

Harry N. Huxhold
Lutheran Book of Worship 288

Contact is still superficial, involving the danger of
yet another servitude. Love alone is capable of unit-
ing living beings in such a way as to complete and
fulfill them, for it alone takes them and joins them by
what is deepest in themselves.

Pierre Teilhard de Chardin (1881-1955)
The Phenomenon of Man
(Harper & Row, 1961), p. 265

In Thornton Wilder's play, "The Skin of Our Teeth," Mrs. Antrobus, near the end, reminds her perennially straying husband of the real basis of their marriage. "I didn't marry you because you were perfect," she tells him. "I didn't even marry you because I loved you. I married you because you gave me a promise." She takes off her wedding band and looks at it. "That promise," she continues, "made up for your faults. And the promise I gave you made up for mine. Two imperfect people got married and it was that promise that made the marriage." Every family consists of "two imperfect people" who have entered into a partnership; and their marriage consists of a promise, not a perfection.

Charles R. Stinnette, Jr.
Grace and the Searching of Our Heart
(Association, 1962), p. 118

When a person lets go of anything—his money, his space, his time, or even his life—he is more likely to refer to what he does as "giving." This allows him to look at the recipient, the person for whom he acts, without ever noticing his own empty hands. The ability to give grows with the riches of selfhood.

Dorothee Sölle
Beyond Mere Obedience
(Augsburg, 1970), p. 53

Almighty God, our heavenly Father,
you set the solitary in families.
We commend to your care
all the homes where your people live.
Keep them, we pray, free from bitterness,
from the thirst for personal victory,
and from pride in self.
Fill them with faith, virtue, knowledge,
moderation, patience, and godliness,
Knit together in enduring affection
those who have become one in marriage.
Amen.

Lutheran Book of Worship
Prayer 230, p. 51

19

Parents and Children

Families today are undergoing great changes. While the "nuclear" family is still common, alongside it are many other forms of family life. The roles of men and women are less predictable and increasingly varied. There is a renewed emphasis on the importance of extended family relationships. Modern methods of birth control have given couples the possibility of having no children at all. When there are children, it is no longer uncommon for a child to live with one parent. What are the responsibilities of parents and children? And what are the particular responsibilities of a Christian parent?

1. What do parents provide for children?

It is no longer possible to assume that a child lives with two parents, a father who works outside the home and a mother who works at home. This idealized picture of family life was never completely accurate, but today it is just one style of family life among many others. Today children are brought up in a variety of settings, with a variety of adult models and types of care.

In spite of this variety, however, the task of child-rearing has not changed greatly. The needs of children have remained much the same. We know a great deal about early childhood development, and we understand how important parents—adult persons who care for children—are.

Social scientists point to the first three to five years of life as the crucial period of a child's development. Much of a child's personality and potential are formed during this time. If a child is without serious handicap and is provided with an emotionally secure and loving environment during these years, he or she will be better equipped to adjust to life.

The first lesson children should learn from life is that no matter what happens, they need not be afraid. Children can learn this only when they feel contented; when they can rely on the care, love, and patience of those on whom they must depend. Security creates confidence. When a feeling of absolute security has been developed during the first year of a child's life, he or she also experiences a sense of well-being. It is out of this deeply-rooted sense of security that children receive the courage to face life.

The early years of childhood are decisive for children. Parents who sacrificially give themselves to their children during these years are irreplaceable. A loving, cooperative, nonhostile relationship has an enormous influence on a child's later ability to deal with life as an adult.

The feelings expressed at home become part of the emotional makeup of a child. Where close parental love for an infant is lacking, the result is often a serious disturbance in later social behavior. Those who have been denied a feeling of security early in life may find it extremely difficult to trust others later.

The task of childrearing is a vital one that deserves the best efforts of parents, both men and women. This task can also be an occupation that makes an enormous contribution both to children and to society. Today's changing roles for women and men have made the division of responsibilities in families very complex. Women, particularly, face great pressures from both traditional expectations that they be mothers and homemakers and expectations that they have jobs and careers outside the home. Both men and women need the freedom to define their roles in a way that respects their own gifts, interests, and responsibilities. Parenthood and the opportunity to pursue a career are rights for both women and men. Yet children also have the right to be cared for, and all parents must take this responsibility seriously.

2. What are the responsibilities of parents and children?

The union of a man and a woman in marriage includes the elements of hope and the future. One of

the privileges of marriage is the opportunity to share in the joys and sorrows of childrearing. Children, however, should not be considered as existing solely for the happiness of their parents; they need to be planned for and cared for. It is an exercise in responsible parenthood to consider carefully the possibilities of having or not having children. To be with children through the years of their development is to experience anew the wonder of every moment of existence, to recapture the spontaneity, creativity, and curiosity we ourselves knew as we grew up.

Every child is a gift, a miracle, a challenging demand, but also a glorious hope and a significant responsibility. With the coming of a child, parents sense that they have been granted a very special opportunity. To bring up a child is to act on God's behalf.

Sometimes the birth of a child is experienced as more pain than joy. Parents may not feel prepared to handle such added responsibility, or the child may have some physical defect. At these times especially, parenthood may seem to be a burden. Yet every child is a gift, someone created in God's image and in need of love. The experience of caring for a child, even when this is difficult, can enrich our lives and strengthen our faith. What may indeed involve great sacrifice may result in still greater joy.

The act of giving one's self to a child is a reflection of the love of God in Jesus Christ. God loves us prior to all our knowledge, thoughts, and decisions. He gives himself to us completely, before we have done anything to deserve such love. Our lives are lived in response to his grace.

The relationship between parents and children, like our relationship with God, involves a lifelong process of giving and receiving. The Fourth Commandment reads, "Honor your father and your mother, that your days may be long in the land which the Lord your God gives you" (Exod. 20:12). Children respond to the love of their parents and return that love. As a family grows together, the bonds of mutual trust and support become stronger, providing a solid foundation for times of stress and difficulty.

Eventually children become independent of their parents, often moving away or getting married, establishing their own living patterns and circles of friends. Yet the relationship between parents and children continues. Love and trust established in the beginning provide ongoing support for each family member. As time goes on, there is often a gradual reversal of roles in which children begin to take on more responsibility for the welfare of their parents. The cycle of life brings growth, change, and the need to make decisions and adapt to new circumstances. Yet through it all the intention of God is honored when both parents and children remain committed to each other's welfare.

Christian parents have some special responsibilities toward their children. Parents should commend their child to God's care and protection and serve as examples of prayer. A good example is more powerful

than many words. There is probably no more effective way for a parent to communicate the reality and presence of God to a child than through prayer. By praying together, the family as a whole finds a refuge and strength and is assured that there is someone who surrounds us and protects us. God is experienced as someone we can call on and trust.

Christian parents will bring their children to worship services and teach them the basics of the Christian faith. They will read to them from the Bible, provide them with copies of the Scriptures, and bring them to Christian instruction classes. They will be open to discussing personal concerns and matters of faith with their children.

The task of parenting is very important and extremely challenging. As in all human relationships, there are problems and frustrations as well as joys and great happiness. No one is a perfect parent or a perfect child. All must work together, bearing with each other in love and forgiveness.

3. What should Christians say about abortion?

Abortion is not the same thing as contraception. Contraception refers to measures taken to prevent the conception of life. An induced abortion always ends a unique human life.

Human life is protected by the Fifth Commandment: "You shall not kill" (Exod. 20:13). Any destruction of human life by human hands is a sign of a tragic disruption of human nature. God wants us to respect life and respect the mystery of life. The life of a fetus is related to the life of its mother, but it is not the same as the life of its mother.

For this reason Christians want to be responsible in their sexual and procreative behavior so as to prevent the temptation to turn to abortion. The widespread practice of abortion today is an irresponsible abuse of God's gift of life and a sign of the sinfulness of humanity and the brokenness of our present social order.

In some circumstances, after all pertinent factors have been responsibly considered, an induced abortion may be a tragic option. Yet the practice of using abortion for personally convenient or selfish reasons must be rejected. Guilt is a common consequence of abortion that applies to all involved—fathers, mothers, doctors, counselors, and the society in which abortion is so readily tolerated.

Because abortion has not only legal and medical, but also theological, ethical, moral, psychological, economic, and social implications, it is too important a decision to be left solely to one person. Those who deal with problem pregnancies should seek out competent Christian guidance to help them explore the entire issue, including long-range effects and options other than abortion.

Summary

- Parents are the single most important influence on children.
- The task of childrearing is a vital one that deserves the best efforts of parents, both men and women.
- Every child is a gift, a miracle, a challenging demand, but also a glorious hope and a significant responsibility.
- The act of giving one's self to a child is a reflection of the love God gives us in Jesus Christ.
- Parents and children need to work together, bearing with each other in love and forgiveness.
- An induced abortion always ends a unique human life, and is a sign of a tragic disruption of human nature.

For reflection

That which we have heard and known,
and what our forefathers have told us,
we will not hide from their children.
We will recount to generations to come
the praiseworthy deeds and the power of the Lord,
and the wonderful works he has done.
He gave his decrees to Jacob
and established a law for Israel,
which he commanded them to teach their children;
that the generations to come might know,

and the children yet unborn;
that they in their turn might tell it to their children;
so that they might put their trust in God,
and not forget the deeds of God,
but keep his commandments. . . .

   Ps. 78:3-7

For the joy of human love,
Brother, sister, parent, child,
Friends on earth and friends above;
For all gentle thoughts and mild:
Christ, our Lord, to you we raise
This our sacrifice of praise.

   Folliott S. Pierpoint (1835-1917)
   Lutheran Book of Worship 561

Do not imagine that the parental office is a matter of your pleasure and whim. It is a strict commandment and injunction of God, who holds you accountable for it.

The trouble is that no one perceives or heeds this. Everybody acts as if God gave us children for our pleasure and amusement. . . .

   Martin Luther (1483-1546)
   Large Catechism, *Book of Concord*
   (Fortress, 1959), p. 388

. Life has taught the rest of us to hold our precious things close . . . . children are likely to give away their most precious things. To those who have made measured generosity a principle of life, the unconsidered generosity of children can be quite unnerving.

Dennis C. Benson and Stan J. Stewart
The Ministry of the Child
(Abingdon, 1979), p. 23

We know, as Christians, that no one is perfect. Not teenagers, not parents. We have no right to expect others to be perfect, and we have no right to let others expect us to fulfill that impossible expectation.

Charles S. Mueller
Getting Along
(Augsburg, 1980), p. 56

Dear Lord,
we pray for our parents first.
Bring mother back to perfect health;
keep father cheerful and vigorous
and let him get good prices for his cocoa.
Make the snakes stay in their holes
when father goes out to work in the morning
and make the girls at home
a little more diligent.

Lord,
keep us studious at Prempeh College
so that we won't disappoint
either You
or our parents.

Lord,
let us be successful
so that the little ones also can go
to a good school.
Kweku wants to become a doctor
and I, an engineer,
to Your honor
and the well-being of our country. . . .

Bless us, Lord,
when father asks for Your blessings.
Amen.

> African prayer, Fritz Pawelzik, ed.
> *I Sing Your Praise All the Day Long*
> (© 1967 by Friendship Press), p. 26
> Used by permission.

20

Work and Rest

Some of the greatest challenges for society today are related to economic life. Daily we face issues of resources, labor, management, production, distribution, unemployment, and leisure time. Economic conflicts lie at the root of many struggles between groups, classes, and nations. The ideologies of capitalism and Marxism are closely intertwined with questions of war and peace. It is essential that Christians bring the insights of faith to bear on modern economic issues as they seek to make responsible decisions in this area.

1. What are the blessings and burdens of work?

Human beings are born into the world in a remarkably undeveloped and defenseless state. We must create what we lack by rearranging the world around us. We build houses, produce clothing, and cultivate land. We are the only living creatures that cook their food. Through our ingenuity we have created an environment of concrete cities, energy networks, traffic control, and waste management that we depend on for our very survival.

Through advancements in technology and the division of labor into various specializations we have been able to bring about an enormous increase in productivity and standard of living. It is no longer possible to conceive of us individually producing everything we possess and consume. We are dependent on complicated and vulnerable social and industrial systems. Technology has increased our independence from the forces of nature, but we have in turn become dependent on technology. Our system of mass production and specialization requires workers to perform the same tasks hundreds or thousands of times each day. The possibility of expressing our creativity through our work has become much more limited. Technological advancement has been both a blessing and a curse.

Work is a basic part of human existence. How persons approach their work reveals a great deal about them. Work has to do with earning a living, the pressures of life, and the content of life. Work has a communal aspect. We can find self-respect and joy through being needed and working with others. We look for praise and recognition to affirm ourselves along with the job we have done.

Work should not be given ultimate value, but neither should it be devalued. Work is important and contributes to self-realization and personal wholeness. This is why working people are bound to their jobs by many different feelings, even when they generally dislike their work. Often they realize this only when they have to retire and leave all their working relationships behind.

God desires that we should work, and that our labor be more than just a means of earning a living. Work is a reflection of and involvement in the creativity of God himself (Gen. 2:1-3). We sometimes experience our work as toil and drudgery (Gen. 3:17-19), but this is not God's intention. Work is intended to be productive and satisfying. It is human sin that distorts work and makes it into a harsh burden.

God's command to human beings was to "subdue" the earth (Gen. 1:28) and to "till" and "keep" the creation (Gen. 2:15). These commands include the instruction to engage in work. Out of responsibility to our Creator we are to manage what he has created. We are called not to exploit the world, but to give it shape and form. When we cease to be good managers of the earth and become merely exploiters of its resources, we are acting out of sin.

During the Middle Ages, the way of life adopted by monks and priests was often described as a "calling." Luther spoke of the calling of every Christian, by which he meant the response in daily life that proceeds out of faith. To see work as a calling or

vocation means to accept responsibility before God for what we do in our work and to understand the role of work in caring for our neighbors. Work prevents chaos, limits our egoism, and provides for the welfare of others. To engage in work is both a right and a responsibility.

2. How are work and rest related?

Life is subject to the rhythm of work and rest. No one can work all the time. The need for sleep and rest is built into human existence. Time is a gift from God that cannot be lengthened or shortened. A day has only 24 hours, yet we can use our time in various ways. It is important for us to strike a balance between work and rest.

Although we now have more leisure time than ever before, we still hear people complain about how little time they have. They rush anxiously from one deadline to another. Self-exertion to the point of burnout may be a symptom both of psychological stress and the inability to rest and relax. We may think we have no time because we fill our days with activities that allow us to avoid ourselves. We would feel better if we used our time more effectively, allowing room not only for work, but also for rest and celebration. If we do not take the time to relax, we will become slaves to our own compulsive drives.

Our personal identity and our worth do not depend on how much we accomplish. When we strive ceaselessly for more and more we find only worry, stress, and exhaustion. Without rest, work can become an oppressive burden. We need time for recreation and reflection. We have a need to be more than productive, to develop our own interests and talents. Leisure time offers the possibility of balancing personal growth with productive work.

God said, "Six days you shall labor, and do all your work; but the seventh day is a sabbath to the Lord your God; in it you shall not do any work" (Exod. 20:9-10). The Third Commandment guards the rhythm of work and rest, labor and worship. Economic activity must not become our god. We need times to rest and to worship our Creator, remembering all that he has done for us.

Most Christians keep Sunday as a day of worship and rest. While the traditional Sabbath commemorated the completion of God's original creation, Sunday, the "Lord's Day," honors God's new creation that began with the resurrection of Jesus Christ. It was on the first day of the week that the women went very early to the tomb and discovered that Jesus had been raised. Christians have kept Sunday as their day of worship from earliest times.

3. How should material possessions be viewed?

The material things we acquire are gifts of God. God provides us with the resources to satisfy our

needs through our labor. The possession of goods provides us with a certain amount of independence. The Seventh Commandment (Exod. 20:15) is concerned principally with the protection of the basic resources of each person.

Possessions may set persons free from need, but they can also be restricting. Things that contribute to life when used responsibly can also become self-destructive when they are misused—that is, when the needs of others are no longer kept in view. People easily become slaves to riches. If we rely on wealth to provide freedom and security, we will only increase our sense of being restricted or confined. We live in a society that encourages possessiveness. Our prestige is largely determined by what "we can afford." The danger we face lies not so much in the goods themselves, but in our own insatiability.

God's command to subdue or manage the earth means that we did not create the world, but we are to care for it. The earth has been entrusted to our care, and we are to manage it responsibly. We must keep in mind not only our own immediate desires, but the intention of the Creator.

We cannot exist without food, clothing, shelter, and tools. We need to acknowledge our need for these basic necessities and also guard against our greed for things we do not need. The story of the tower of Babel shows how work is often done not out of obedience to God's commands and intentions, but out of an obsession with prestige and power (Gen. 11:

1-9). It is human greed that leads to our exploitation of the earth and the deprivation of our fellow human beings (Luke 12:16-21).

According to the Bible, God is concerned about what we do with the material possessions we have received. Everything we have is a loan from God: "The earth is the Lord's and all that is in it" (Ps. 24:1). Everything belongs to God, and we are to manage what he has loaned us according to his will.

As managers rather than owners of our possessions we recognize that these are intended not merely for our own enjoyment, but also for the good of others. God calls us to provide for the needs of all people out of the abundant resources he has given us. Our world includes hundreds of millions of people who do not have even the bare necessities of life. Their poverty stands in sharp contrast to the wealth and luxury of the developed nations. This unjust situation needs to be addressed and corrected. Taxes that are paid to support various governmental programs provide some help, as do the contributions made to the church and various social agencies. Christians support both emergency relief and self-development projects, even as they work toward the realization of a more just economic order.

4. What are the challenges of modern economic life?

The process of industrialization has brought great benefits to human beings, but it has also brought great suffering. The industrial revolution aroused widespread criticism because of the way factory work often manipulated, dehumanized, and victimized workers. Many people who needed work left rural environments and traditional social structures to find employment in the industrialized urban centers. Wages, working conditions, and living arrangements were often seriously deficient in the cities. The human costs of increased productivity were high.

One of the first serious thinkers to address the abuses of industrialization was Karl Marx (1818-1883). Marx analyzed the structure of capitalist society and concluded that the working class was being exploited—and deprived of the fruits of its labor—by those who owned and controlled the means of production. He believed that the history of economic life could be understood in terms of conflict between classes, and the modern conflict between the working class and the capitalist class would be resolved when ownership of the means of production passed into the hands of the masses.

The introduction of some ideas advanced by Marx has had great impact on modern economic life. His understanding of the problems related to industrial society has been applied to economic structures in various ways. Some countries have assumed state control over all means of production within a tightly-regulated political structure. Other countries have placed the control of major industries in the hands of the state, while emphasizing the democratic process and allowing some room for private initiative. In countries where Communism and socialism have not been welcomed, labor organizations have developed into strong advocates of the rights of workers, and many abuses have been eliminated.

There are various ways in which Christians view our modern economic structures. Some Christians believe that economic justice will not come simply through appealing to the good will of individuals. They propose a transformation of basic economic structures, as has already happened in some democratic European countries where the state has assumed control of major industries.

Other Christians believe the capitalist system can provide for the welfare of all people in society if only it is allowed to do so. They propose that a more equitable distribution of wealth can come about through such means as tax policy, government loans, investment incentives, and legislation against monopolies.

In some countries there have been experiments with economic alternatives other than socialism and capitalism. Some corporations have moved toward increased employee participation in ownership, operation, and profit. Joint participation in management provides a way to defuse some of the conflict between labor and management without eliminating private ownership. There have also been some experiments in running businesses cooperatively. Cooperatives attempt to break down the distinction between producer and consumer.

When discussing the thought of Karl Marx, it is helpful to distinguish between his analysis of the problems in industrial society and his prescriptions for a solution. Marx may have been correct in saying that our technological society, based on a division of labor, has led to structures that force persons into new forms of dependency. But it is doubtful whether the abolition of private ownership of the means of production can, in and of itself, solve the problems he identified. In fact, in some countries the abolition of private ownership has been tied to totalitarian political structures that have actually *increased* the powerlessness of the working class. The interrelationships between the economic and political arenas are very complex, and there is no simple panacea that will usher in an era of perfect justice. When structural change is needed, it must be very carefully planned so that it avoids other serious pitfalls. The persistence of economic problems in both capitalist and socialist countries raises the question whether the industrial process itself may have some serious shortcomings. Could it be that the size and impersonality of modern industry has negative consequences for society, regardless of the economic structure?

Many countries in the world are only now beginning the process of industrialization. These are often

referred to as "third world" nations. The "first world" is the industrialized and capitalistic West, and the "second world" is the industrialized and Marxist East. In addition, some people speak of a "fourth world," those nations that are most resource poor and are experiencing acute crises of poverty and hunger.

Until recently it was thought that the problems of the third and fourth worlds could be solved simply through industrialization along either the capitalist or socialist models. Today there is wide recognition that worldwide industrialization poses severe problems. The process of industrialization undermines traditional family and social structures in favor of individualism, and material values are emphasized at the expense of deeper human values. Further, the energy, water, and mineral resources required for large-scale industry are becoming ever more scarce, and there is a question as to how much more environmental contamination the earth can tolerate. It is clear that the world could not sustain human life if every person had the standard of living of an average European or American.

Some people have suggested that the poor will have to remain poor so that the rich nations can enjoy their privileges. Christians oppose such thinking as contrary to the entire biblical tradition. Our current environmental problems have not been caused by the poor, but by the wealthy. There is substantial evidence to indicate that poverty is actually increasing *because of* industrialization. The developed nations can only support their present standard of living by obtaining inexpensive labor and raw materials from the less-developed countries, while the benefits of third world industrialization have often been limited to elite classes. The economic level of poor persons moving from agricultural to urban settings often declines even more, for the degrading conditions Marx observed over a century ago in Europe's industrial centers are now repeated in many parts of the third world.

Some people have suggested that the search for economic justice focus less on production and more on distribution. It is claimed that God has provided enough resources for all to enjoy, if only the rich will give up their economic power over the poor, waste less, and live simpler life-styles. A reduced level of consumption by the developed nations is seen as the only real hope of avoiding environmental and political disaster.

There is a relationship between poverty and political instability in the third world. Hunger, powerlessness, repression, and despair are bound up with violence and revolution. Some representatives from the third world insist that real peace will require a just international economic order. So long as economic issues are not seriously addressed, they see little hope of maintaining long-term political stability in their countries.

Summary

● Work is intended to be productive and satisfying. It is human sin that distorts work and makes it into a harsh burden.

● The need for sleep and rest is built into human existence. If we do not take the time to relax, we will become slaves to our own compulsive drives.

● The Third Commandment guards the rhythm of work and rest, labor and worship.

● Things that contribute to life when used responsibly can also become self-destructive when the needs of others are no longer kept in view.

● Everything belongs to God, and we are to manage what he has loaned us according to his will.

● The persistence of economic problems in both capitalist and socialist countries raises the question whether the industrial process itself has some serious shortcomings.

For reflection

Give me neither poverty nor riches; feed me with the food that is needful for me, lest I be full, and deny thee, and say, "Who is the Lord?" or lest I be poor, and steal, and profane the name of my God.

Prov. 30:8-9

Forth in thy name, O Lord, I go,
My daily labor to pursue;
Thee, only thee, resolved to know
In all I think or speak or do.

The task thy wisdom has assigned,
Oh, let me cheerfully fulfill;
In all my works thy presence find,
And prove thy good and perfect will.

Thee may I set at my right hand,
Whose eyes my inmost substance see,
And labor on at thy command,
And offer all my works to thee.

Charles Wesley (1707-1788)
Lutheran Book of Worship 505

Labor is a person's *just right,* but it is not one's *justification.* Our welfare is at stake in our productivity, but not our salvation. Profit is a sign of what is often our ambiguous success in the world of mankind, but not in the kingdom of God. If these distinctions are neglected—if that which is penultimate is made ultimate—then an atmosphere results in which works become works righteousness, productivity becomes religion, and performance becomes the ideology of performance. This leads to an idolatry of economics, along with an alienated, one-dimensional world in which people are made into means of production.

Jan Milič Lochman
Living Roots of Reformation
(Augsburg, 1979), p. 31

The system of liberal capitalism and the temptation of the Marxist system would appear to exhaust the possibilities of transforming the economic structures of our continent. Both systems militate against the dignity of the human person.

Second General Conference of Latin American
    Bishops, Medellin, Colombia, 1968
The Church in the Present-Day Transformation of Latin America in the Light of the Council
(Division for Latin America, U.S.C.C.), vol. 2, p. 45

In the developing countries people are not only asking for food, but are also demanding liberty, independence, justice, equal opportunity, genuine human dignity, and full participation in the determining of their own lives.

This means that wherever we confront oppression, and the dehumanization of human life, there we are dealing with underdevelopment—the underdevelopment of which plenty can be found in the "developed" countries! When we talk about development, then, we are not simply discussing economic realities, but those that concern the totality of human need. Nor are we simply talking about those countries conventionally considered "underdeveloped."

Fridolin Ukur
What Asian Christians Are Thinking
(New Day, 1976), p. 293

Lord, let me see the meaning of things
so I can get involved.
Let me see the meaning of the food
and join those who produce. . . .
Let me know the meaning of politics
and join the lawmakers.
Let me know the meaning of housing
and join the planners.
Let me know the meaning of theater
and join the actors.
Lord,
let me get involved,
by looking for the meaning
under the work of people.
Help me ask
why—
why people invent,
act, produce food, and plan.
If I know the meaning

of what I do,
I can do it with gladness, Jesus.

Herbert F. Brokering
Surprise Me, Jesus
(Augsburg, 1973), p. 52

21

Government and Human Rights

Justice and the observance of human rights are important parts of God's intention for life. Again and again the Scriptures yoke righteousness with peace, peace with justice, and justice with the recognition of the rights, freedoms, and responsibilities of persons.

Government has an important role in preserving justice and human rights. Government is an essential part of all human society that should protect persons from oppression and manipulation by others. Although government cannot fully establish God's kingdom, God intends it to be an instrument of justice in the world. How should Christians relate to government? How should Christians work for human rights?

1. What should be the relationship between Christians and the government?

Christians have lived under many different forms of government. Because the proper function of the state is the preservation of life, Christians should normally obey those in authority, "not only to avoid

God's wrath but also for the sake of conscience" (Rom. 13:5). This is why Paul could say, "Let every person be subject to the governing authorities" (Rom. 13:1).

Yet the authority of the state is not absolute. When government attempts to force persons to disobey God, Christians must disobey the government. The book of Acts reports that Peter and the other apostles were accused of continuing to proclaim the gospel even when they had been strictly charged not to. They told the authorities, "We must obey God rather than men" (Acts 5:29). The New Testament recognizes that the state can sometimes assume excessive power and become an instrument of evil. The book of Revelation presents a dramatic picture of the church suffering under such a government and portrays the final victory of God over all human power and arrogance.

The First Commandment prevents Christians from giving ultimate authority to any government. Such power belongs to God alone. Yet Christians recognize the need for order in society and so respect the function of government in promoting the welfare of persons. Christians have a critical perspective that excludes glorification of the state and yet respects the benefits government can bring.

2. What should be the relationship between church and state?

A healthy relationship between the church and the government could be expressed as institutional separation and functional interaction. Government should safeguard the rights of all persons and groups in society to the free exercise of their religious beliefs, worship practices, and organizational arrangements within the laws of morality, human rights, and property. The government should not make any decisions regarding the validity or orthodoxy of any doctrine, recognizing that it is the province of religious groups to state their doctrines, determine forms of organization, train leaders, conduct worship, and carry on mission and ministry without undue interference from or entanglement with government.

Government's distinctive calling is to maintain peace, establish justice, protect and advance human rights, and promote the general welfare of all persons. Government has the authority and power to ensure that individuals and groups, including religious communities and their agencies, adhere to the civil law. Government enters into relationships, associations, and organizational arrangements with nongovernmental groups, including churches, according to a nation's laws and traditions, in order to fulfill its God-given calling and without compromising or inhibiting the integrity of either the groups or the government.

The functional interaction between the government and religious bodies is in areas of mutual endeavor, where such interaction assists in the maintenance of good order, the protection and extension of civil rights, the establishment of social justice and equality of opportunity, the promotion of the general welfare, and the advancement of the dignity of all persons. This principle underscores the fact that God rules both the civil and spiritual dimensions of life, making it appropriate for the government and the churches to relate creatively and responsibly to each other.

In this functional interaction, the government may conclude that efforts and programs of the churches provide services of broad social benefit. In such instances the government may offer and the churches may accept various forms of assistance to furnish the services. Functional interaction also includes the roles of the churches in informing persons about, advocating for, and speaking publicly on issues and proposals related to social justice and human rights.

3. How should Christians work for human rights?

All human beings have certain basic needs:

- food, shelter, and clothing
- love and the opportunity to express love
- recognition as a unique person
- structures of family relationships
- the exchange of goods and services
- life under an orderly system

These common human needs were recognized by the Universal Declaration of Human Rights, passed

by the General Assembly of the United Nations in 1948. This Declaration, and other human rights initiatives taken by the United Nations, incorporate the following:

- respect for the essential dignity and integrity of each person
- guarantee of freedom of expression and responsible decision making
- assurance of opportunity for each person to develop freely and fully that person's unique potential
- provisions for participation in the institutions and relationships of one's society
- protection against arbitrary and despotic uses of power

Christians support the intent of the Universal Declaration and the covenants based on them. When human rights are denied, Christians press for their recognition. Where they are recognized, Christians insist that they be upheld.

Little progress is likely to be made in assuring human rights unless economic strength and political viability can be achieved. Economic, political, and social development become crucial for peace, justice, and human rights. The less developed nations need help in developing their own foundations for economic strength, political viability, and effective social systems. Such efforts must be genuinely international in character. There no longer is room for a strong nation to impose its economic, political, or social systems on another. Nations, like persons, seek their own integrity.

Action for peace, justice, and human rights opposes many entrenched institutional forces. Various organized forces thrive on aggression, conquest, intimidation, exploitation, disorder, preferential position, or the denial of justice and human rights. Economic, political, and social systems in their operations at home and abroad often intensify the difficulties. Christians recognize the hard realities of the human situation. Yet they have a vision of the world as God sees it. They affirm the lordship of Jesus Christ and his triumph over all the forces of evil.

4. What should Christians say about women's rights?

We live in a time when the roles of women in society are changing. Many strides have been made to recognize the rights of women. These steps are matters of simple justice and equity.

God created all human beings in his image. Some he created female, some male. Though each person bears some bodily traits of the other sex, each person is known as female or male. Through training and in living together we encounter the customs, roles, and rules of the communities in which we live, and we learn what is expected of female and male. Some qualities are thought of as masculine and some as feminine. Yet these are *human* qualities found in varying degrees in each person, whether female or male. The deeper meaning of our God-given sexuality, which both separates us and attracts us, remains a profound mystery. We do not try to fathom this mystery. Rather, we accept and celebrate the mystery of our femaleness and maleness as one of God's gifts.

Under the impact of massive social change the traditional role definitions are breaking down. No longer need women so predominantly find their identity through their roles in their families, men through their roles in their jobs. Both women and men now are seeking for identity, for recognition, and for integrity in new roles, new spheres, new relationships. Both women and men struggle with stereotypes, customs, and practices that raise artificial barriers against finding their identity and fulfilling their selfhood.

The changing roles of women and men have particular impact on families. Through creation God has indeed assigned the childbearing role to women. However, the important tasks associated with child nurture—providing the physical and emotional necessities, and fostering the development of a child into a mature adult—require the efforts of men as well as of women. Family living should be an example of love, respect, commitment, sharing, caring, choice, and service.

Every social institution is affected by the growing realization that women have rights, abilities, and responsibilities for participating in the whole of life. Opportunities once limited to men are opening to women. Opportunities once regarded as "women's work" are opening to men. Standards for hours and conditions of work, for pay, for promotions and advancement, for valuing services to the community, and for legal rights, for example, will be affected. The gifts of both women and men help make up the wholeness of our human community.

Christians examine critically the competing claims as to the rightful roles and responsibilities of men and women in church and society. They exercise judgment on what is beneficial and what is detrimental to persons, to families, and to the abilities of social structures to meet human needs.

4. What should Christians say about racism?

Racism is one of the most destructive sins in today's world. It refuses to honor God's acts in creation, redemption, and sanctification. Racism builds on human pride and prejudice and abuses power for selfish advantage. Racism dishonors God, our neighbors, and ourselves. It rejects the meaning of God's becoming incarnate in Jesus Christ, because if we reject another person we reject Jesus Christ.

The sin of racism expresses itself in many ways. It may be harsh and blatant; it can be patronizing or cloaked in euphemisms. It may be so open and exposed that no one can miss it; it may be so subtle and covered over that only the victims feel its destructiveness.

Pride in the presumed superiority of members of one race over those of another provides a foundation for racism. Power exerted by the dominant group through its control of the institutions, systems, resources, and customs of that society enforces its prejudices and reinforces the structures of racism. Members of the subordinate group are assumed to have neither the full humanity nor wisdom nor good judgment to make decisions affecting their lives. It is assumed that important decisions must be made for them, not by them. Their dependency grows as their freedom and responsibility are denied. Racism destroys the dignity, integrity, and positive self-image of human beings created in the image of the living God. Racism spawns fear, guilt, frustration, hostility, and violence.

In the past people assumed the rightness of segregation—of separate but "equal" facilities, reservations, restrictive covenants, and limited opportunities for separate development by members of subordinate racial groups. Later, integration became the key legal word. In its practical effects, however, integration meant that minority persons were expected to take on the values, goals, life-styles, and culture of the dominant majority. This is a denial of the humanity of persons who take pride in their own ethnic identity and integrity.

In response to the gospel, our emphasis should be on recognizing and rejoicing in the diversity and variety of experiences among human beings. The integrity and aspirations of members of minority groups as persons and as members of the honored ethnic groups are respected. On this basis Christians continue to support the equal rights and equal opportunities of all persons, regardless of racial or ethnic background. At the same time, Christians rejoice in the gospel that breaks down all barriers between persons and unites all believers into the family of God: "There is neither Jew nor Greek, there is neither slave nor free, there is neither male nor female; for you are all one in Christ Jesus" (Gal. 3:28).

Summary

● A healthy relationship between the church and the government could be expressed as institutional separation and functional interaction.

● When human rights are denied, Christians press for their recognition. Where such rights are recognized, Christians insist that they be upheld.

● Recognizing the rights of women is a matter of justice and equity.

● Both women and men struggle with stereotypes, customs, and practices that raise artificial barriers against finding their identity and fulfilling their selfhood.

● Our emphasis should be on recognizing and rejoicing in the diversity and variety of experiences among human beings.

● Christians rejoice in the gospel that breaks down

all barriers between persons and unites all believers into the family of God.

For reflection

And he came to Nazareth, where he had been brought up; and he went to the synagogue, as his custom was, on the sabbath day. And he stood up to read; and there was given to him the book of the prophet Isaiah. He opened the book and found the place where it was written,

The Spirit of the Lord is upon me,
because he has anointed me to preach good news to
the poor.
He has sent me to proclaim release to the captives
and recovering of sight to the blind,
to set at liberty those who are oppressed,
to proclaim the acceptable year of the Lord.

And he closed the book, and gave it back to the attendant, and sat down; and the eyes of all in the synagogue were fixed on him. And he began to say to them, "Today this scripture has been fulfilled in your hearing."

Luke 4:16-21

God the Almighty has made our rulers mad; they actually think they can do—and order their subjects to do—whatever they please. And the subjects make the mistake of believing that they, in turn, are bound to obey their rulers in everything. It has gone so far that the rulers have begun ordering the people to get rid of certain books, and to believe and conform to what the rulers prescribe. They are thereby presumptuously setting themselves in God's place, lording it over men's consciences and faith, and schooling the Holy Spirit according to their own crackbrained ideas. Nevertheless, they let it be known that they are not to be contradicted, and are to be called gracious lords all the same.

They issue public proclamations, and say that this is the emperor's command and that they want to be obedient Christian princes, just as if they really meant it and no one noticed the scoundrel behind the mask. If the emperor were to take a castle or a city from them or command some other injustices, we should then see how quickly they would find themselves obliged to resist the emperor and disobey him. But when it comes to fleecing the poor or venting their spite on the word of God, it becomes a matter of "obedience to the imperial command." Such people were formerly called scoundrels; now they have to be called obedient Christian princes.

Martin Luther (1483-1546)
Luther's Works, vol. 45, II
(Fortress, 1962), pp. 83-84

We hold these truths to be self-evident, that all men are created equal, that they are endowed by their Creator with certain unalienable Rights, that among these are Life, Liberty, and the pursuit of Happiness. —That to secure these rights, Governments are instituted among Men, deriving their just powers from the consent of the governed,—That whenever any Form of Government becomes destructive of these ends, it is the Right of the People to alter or to abolish it, and to institute new Government, laying its foundation on such principles and organizing its powers in such form, as to them shall seem most likely to effect their Safety and Happiness. Prudence, indeed, will dictate that Governments long established should not be changed for light and transient causes; and accordingly all experience hath shown, that mankind are more disposed to suffer, while evils are sufferable, than to right themselves by abolishing the forms to which they are accustomed. But when a long train of abuses and usurpations, pursuing invariably the same Object evinces a design to reduce them under absolute Despotism, it is their right, it is their duty, to throw off such Government, and to provide new Guards for their future security.

United States Declaration of Independence

Christians affirm the utterly singular and sacred status of the human person. Our relationship with God himself is reflected in the manner of our relating to other persons. The rights possessed by human beings are to be revered, Christians assert, because they are ontologically based, they are a gift rooted in the very Being of the Creator. Human rights are not privileges that can be bestowed or withdrawn by any human agency, including the state. Society can and must limit the exercise of human rights, but only for the most compelling reasons that must always be subject to examination.

Richard John Neuhaus
Christian Faith and Public Policy
(Augsburg, 1977), p. 102

I have a dream that one day on the red hills of Georgia the sons of former slaves and the sons of former slaveowners will be able to sit down together at the table of brotherhood.

I have a dream that one day even the state of Mississippi, a state sweltering with the people's injustice, sweltering with the heat of oppression, will be transformed into an oasis of freedom and justice.

I have a dream that my four little children will one day live in a nation where they will not be judged by the color of their skin, but by the content of their character.

This is our hope. This is the faith that I go back to

the South with—with this faith we will be able to
hew out of the mountain of despair a stone of hope.

Martin Luther King Jr. (1929-1968)
August 28, 1963
Washington, D.C.

Judge eternal, throned in splendor,
Lord of lords and King of kings,
With your living fire of judgment
Purge this land of bitter things;
Solace all its wide dominion
With the healing of your wings.

Crown, O God, your own endeavor;
Cleave our darkness with your sword;
Feed the faint and hungry peoples
With the richness of your Word;
Cleanse the body of this nation
Through the glory of the Lord.

Henry S. Holland (1847-1918)
Lutheran Book of Worship 418

Part Seven

Where Are We Going?

It has become evident that, while we may be able to survive some of the thunder clouds that loom threatening on the horizon of history, lasting hope cannot come from within us. While we can always achieve temporary victories, ultimately death will stare us in the face. When we give account of the hope that is in us, we can only do so because it has been placed in us from beyond our time-bound world. Any tenable hope for the future thus cannot rest on us but must be affirmed by the God who created the world, does sustain it, and will eventually redeem it.

Hans Schwarz
On the Way to the Future
(Augsburg, 1979), p. 162

22

Today and Tomorrow

After he was baptized by John the Baptist, Jesus announced, "The time is fulfilled, and the kingdom of God is at hand; repent, and believe in the gospel" (Mark 1:15). His last earthly conversations also dealt with the kingdom of God (Acts 1:3). He taught his disciples to pray that the kingdom would come (Matt. 6:10; Luke 11:2), told parables about the kingdom, and commissioned his disciples to preach about the kingdom.

Over the centuries, this expectation of God's kingdom has not always been emphasized. Where the dramatic and climactic involvement of God with the world has been talked about, such discussions have often taken the form of bizarre and irresponsible speculations about the future that few people could take seriously. In the meantime, various political philosophies have arisen that proclaim the advent of the human kingdom. How are the proclamation of the kingdom of God and the improvement of present social conditions related?

1. What is the kingdom of God?

In the New Testament the terms "kingdom of God" and "kingdom of heaven" refer to the kingly rule of God over the entire world (Matt. 4:17; Mark 1:15). The Old Testament had expressed the hope for the establishment of God's reign in various ways. What was new in Jesus' proclamation was the claim that the future was now "at hand." The kingdom comes where Jesus Christ is (Luke 17:21). He brings God's kingdom by forgiving sin, conquering evil, and making it possible for persons to participate in the life of the kingdom. He is the Judge of the world, the one who has initiated and will complete God's reign.

We can summarize the implications of the New Testament message about the kingdom of God in the following way:

● The kingdom is a present reality as well as a future reality. It enters the world and takes hold of persons. The kingdom is here in this present world.

● The kingdom will come to fulfillment in the future. It will encompass all things in a new state of affairs. Suffering and pain, sin and death, evil and demonic powers will no longer exist.

● The kingdom comes in surprising and hidden ways. It appears precisely in the places where there is blindness, lameness, leprosy, and death. It manifests itself where it is least expected. It is hidden in the cross of Jesus.

- The kingdom is characterized by struggle, not by easy progress in the world. God's kingdom comes whenever evil is confronted and conquered.
- The kingdom of God can neither be identified with nor separated from the church. The church is the vanguard of God's kingdom on earth. It is the communion of disciples authorized to proclaim the kingdom's coming. The body of Christ is engaged in direct combat with the principalities and powers aligned against God.

Christians live "in the world" but are not "of the world" (John 17). They view reality from a new perspective, from the perspective of God's kingdom. Through faith they see the threads of God's new creation woven in, with, and through the tapestry of time and history, in social change and personal renewal.

Christians belong to God and are dependent on him. Yet they are called to be part of God's shaping of the world. As Paul wrote, "all things are yours . . . and you are Christ's; and Christ is God's" (1 Cor. 3:21-23).

The world cannot be cured of all its ills by the application of a single principle, as some political philosophies would have us believe. According to the Bible, reality has several dimensions. It must be understood within the tension of different perspectives:

- *preservation* of the world and *redemption* of the world

- *sinfulness* and *sainthood* of Christians
- the *beginning* of the kingdom now and the *fulfillment* of the kingdom still to come

Christians live in the tension between the present and the future, today and tomorrow, believing and seeing. This tension finds its resolution in Jesus Christ, who holds all things together (Col. 1:17). He is the human being who is also God, the one who died and rose again, the one who came and will come again.

2. How are change and renewal related to the kingdom?

God is the source of both personal renewal and social change. Only the Creator can create something truly new in place of what already exists. We are involved in his acts of re-creation. The coming of his kingdom affects marriage, family life, occupations, economies, traditions, cultures, and nations.

God's kingdom comes to us through the proclamation of the gospel, which is good news for individuals and for society as a whole. The gospel has effects in the political realm, yet it refuses to become the servant of particular political purposes and interests. The gospel cannot be measured by political successes or failures. The work of the gospel extends beyond political change and includes the re-creation of all things.

Political change and personal renewal should not be

set over against each other. If we place social change above all else, we can easily fall prey to a dictatorship of expediency that politicizes all areas of life. On the other hand, when personal renewal becomes our only concern, the will of God related to social justice is neglected. Both individual well-being and community wholeness are promoted and established by the gospel.

Plans and programs for changing the structures of society are as common as human hope itself. We all long for the fulfillment of history, and we seek ways to improve our lives and promote justice. One method by which we try to improve conditions of life is education. Christians have placed great emphasis on education, yet education alone is not sufficient to transform life. Knowledge can be put to either good or evil uses, and any attempt to change human beings that fails to take sin into account will result in only superficial modifications. Change requires not only knowledge but also trust, communication, and community.

The tension between the present reality of God's kingdom and its future fulfillment results in a similar tension within Christian ethics. Because the kingdom is here already, Christians show the fruits of their faith in acts of love and justice. They work to make the structures of society reflect God's will. At the same time, believers know God's kingdom will not be fulfilled within history, but only on the "edge" or "horizon" of history, when Christ returns to complete all he has begun. For this reason all personal and social

reform has an unfinished quality. The lingering presence of sin resists all perfectionistic schemes of human development. The final fulfillment of human history will not be accomplished by anyone except Christ, when he returns as King and Judge of the world. Christians maintain a healthy skepticism about proposals to solve all human problems, even as they work to express love and establish justice in God's world.

Summary

● Jesus brings God's kingdom by forgiving sin, conquering evil, and making it possible for persons to participate in the life of the kingdom.

● Christians view reality from the new perspective of God's kingdom.

● The world cannot be cured of all its ills by the application of a single principle, as some political philosophies would have us believe.

● Christians live in the tension between the present and the future, today and tomorrow, believing and seeing.

● The gospel is good news both for individuals and for society as a whole. Political change and personal renewal should not be set over against each other.

● Christians maintain a healthy skepticism about proposals to solve all human problems, even as they work to express love and establish justice in God's world.

For reflection

It shall come to pass in the latter days
that the mountain of the house of the Lord
shall be established as the highest of the mountains,
and shall be raised above the hills;
and all the nations shall flow to it,
and many peoples shall come, and say:
"Come, let us go up to the mountain of the Lord,
to the house of the God of Jacob;
that he may teach us his ways
and that we may walk in his paths."
For out of Zion shall go forth the law,
and the word of the Lord from Jerusalem.
He shall judge between the nations,
and shall decide for many peoples;
and they shall beat their swords into plowshares,
and their spears into pruning hooks;
nation shall not lift up sword against nation,
neither shall they learn war any more.

Isa. 2:2-4

Come, thou long-expected Jesus,
Born to set thy people free;
From our fears and sins release us;
Let us find our rest in thee.
Israel's strength and consolation,
Hope of all the earth thou art,

Dear desire of ev'ry nation,
Joy of ev'ry longing heart.

Charles Wesley (1707-1788)
Lutheran Book of Worship 30

There is as great a difference between changing a
government and improving it as the distance from
heaven to earth. It is easy to change a government,
but it is difficult to get one that is better, and the
danger is that you will not.

Martin Luther (1483-1546)
Luther's Works, vol. 46, III
(Fortress, 1967), pp. 111-112

Hope for an otherwordly future need not be a seda-
tive but may be a stimulant to action. The Christian
church is to a large extent responsible for the revolutionary consciousness that is emerging around the
world. Indirectly, through centuries of ministry and
missionary activity, the church itself has provoked
liberation consciousness by preaching a message that
sets things in motion by stirring the imagination,
arousing new expectations, and stimulating a crusad-
ing zeal to translate hopes, whose realization some
would postpone for heaven above, into the social
structures of this world now.

Ted Peters
Futures, Human and Divine
(John Knox, 1978), pp. 168-169

To the victims of a system of rampant injustice it
is equally important to realize that God is also the
God of power, not only the God who will lead them
to freedom. He is a God in charge in his universe. He
is not impotent despite all appearances to the contrary, despite the fact that evil and injustice seem to
be on the ascendant. He is Lord, the all-ruler of the
book of Daniel and the Revelation of St. John the
Divine. Nothing that happens can ever catch him off
guard. He is not like the gods of the prophets of Baal
whom Elijah mocked so cruelly. He has not fallen
asleep, or gone on a journey, or turned aside to relieve
himself so that our cries rise into an empty void; our
cries do not fall on deaf or unheeding ears. No, our
God has heard and seen our affliction and has come
down to deliver us. And he is strong to save.

Bishop Desmond Tutu
African Theology en Route
(Orbis, 1979), p. 166

Almighty God,
you once called John the Baptist
to give witness to the coming of your Son

and to prepare his way.
Grant us, your people,
the wisdom to see your purpose today
and the openness to hear your will,
that we may witness to Christ's coming
and so prepare his way;
through Jesus Christ our Lord,
who lives and reigns
with you and the Holy Spirit,
one God, now and forever.
Amen.

Lutheran Book of Worship
Prayer for the Third Sunday in Advent

23

Death and Dying

We do not like to talk about death. In fact, we try to avoid the subject as much as possible. Most deaths occur in hospitals, far removed from the normal flow of life. When we have to talk about someone who has died, we say they have "departed" or "passed away." We are sensitive about death because we fear it. It is unpredictable, and it threatens us and those closest to us.

In recent years there has been an emphasis on dealing more openly with death and dying. Studies have shown that those who expect their own death or experience the death of a loved one go through various stages of rejection and acceptance. We are told that death is natural and we must be prepared to deal with it. What is the meaning of death? How can Christian faith help us relate to those who are dying?

1. What does the Bible say about death?

The Bible sees death as neither a trivial matter nor as the greatest possible disaster. Death can sometimes be very frightening (Pss. 18:4-5; 116:2-3). Death is an enemy—indeed the "last enemy" (1 Cor. 15:26), but it will be conquered (1 Cor. 15:54-55).

The people of Israel did not make death an object of devotion, as did some ancient peoples, particularly the Egyptians. The Old Testament says human beings are created from the earth and return to the earth (Gen. 3:19). When his time to die drew near, King David said, "I am about to go the way of all the earth" (1 Kings 2:1-2). When Abraham died, he had lived a full life and was of "a good old age" (Gen. 25:8). The Old Testament understands death to be a punishment from God only when it is untimely or violent.

Nevertheless, in the Old Testament death is still seen as threatening a person's relationship with God because the dead were thought to be separated from God: "Sheol cannot thank thee, death cannot praise thee; those who go down to the pit cannot hope for thy faithfulness. The living, the living, he thanks thee, as I do this day" (Isa. 38:18-19). In the view of the Old Testament, it is the possibility of being separated from God that makes dying so difficult.

Within the Old Testament, hope beyond death is an intuition that does not come to full expression. The faith of a person in the power of God does offer a glimmer of hope, however: "Though my flesh and my heart should waste away, God is the strength of my heart and my portion forever" (Ps. 73:26); "He will

375 DEATH AND DYING

swallow up death for ever, and the Lord God will wipe away tears from all faces" (Isa. 25:8).

The New Testament clearly affirms that death is not the end. Jesus said, "he is not God of the dead, but of the living; for all live to him" (Luke 20:38). The first Christians expected to be with Christ immediately after death (Phil. 1:23). Death would not separate them from the love of God in Jesus Christ (Rom. 8:38-39). Those who believe already share in a life that is eternal: "he who believes in me, though he die, yet shall he live" (John 11:25). The dead do not cease to exist; they are kept safely in Gods' hand.

2. How can we deal with death and dying?

Our psychological reactions to death and dying are complex. Several stages are usually involved, though their exact duration and sequence vary depending on the person and the circumstances. In her book *On Death and Dying* (Macmillan, 1969), Elisabeth Kübler-Ross identifies the following stages:

- denial and isolation
- anger
- bargaining
- depression
- acceptance

At first the possibility of dying is denied and suppressed. This is followed by a mistrust of relatives

who seem withdrawn and appear to know more than they say. Patients often express their anger at the threat of death. They may attempt to bargain with God or their doctors to try to extend their lives. Soon despondency and fear take hold. Resistance lessens. Sleeplessness and troubling dreams may occur. Physically and mentally exhausted, the patient usually accepts impending death.

In recent years there have been a number of cases in which persons who were clinically dead—that is, whose hearts had stopped—were resuscitated. Some of those who have revived speak of having had intense experiences, impressions of great beauty and profound peace. They found the experience of waking to be an unsettling disruption. It is also true that some individuals have reported having frightening and troubling experiences, and others could remember nothing.

Is this evidence for life after death? It is too early to draw such a conclusion. Those who are clinically dead are not yet biologically dead, and we do not yet have a very clear understanding of what physically happens in such circumstances.

Sooner or later each of us will die. Death is a reality that casts its shadow over all of life. We cannot "practice" dying, but it is important that we be prepared for death, in the spirit of Psalm 90: "So teach us to number our days, that we may apply our hearts to wisdom" (v. 12). Prayer can help us assess ourselves realistically and use our time more effectively. It can also preserve us from overestimating such things as worldly success, happiness, and youth. By learning to die, we are learning to live.

Nothing can better prepare us for death than a life lived in response to the gospel. There are a number of things we can do on a regular basis to prepare ourselves for death, as well as for life. Among them are these:

- use every moment, hour, and day wisely
- allow time for work, planning, conversation, reflection, play, rest, and sleep
- pay attention to what our conscience tells us
- deal with conflict in a prompt and constructive way
- forgive others and ask them to forgive us
- be willing to part with everything we have for the sake of others
- give thanks for each day God gives us
- be reminded of the hope of the resurrection in Christ

3. How can we help those who are dying?

It is extremely important that those who are dying not be left alone on the last part of their life journey. Those who are seriously ill—whether at home, in nursing homes, or in hospitals—know when their condition is growing worse. They will ask doctors, nurses, relatives, and pastors to tell them whether or not they are dying. The truth should not be kept from them. It is

best when all the persons involved in the care of a dying patient work together to help that individual deal with his or her possible death.

Often it is impossible to carry on a conversation with an ill person because of the effects of pain-killing or sleep-inducing drugs. Yet frequently a patient can hear everything that is said in his or her presence, and may retain hearing and comprehension to the very moment of death. Those who care for the dying must take this into account. A person who does not appear to be able to respond can still be greatly helped by prayer and words of encouragement, or greatly hurt by insensitive conversation.

Those who suffer from life-threatening illnesses need persons with whom they can share their concerns, including questions of faith. They may feel the need to set things in order and make up for past failures. They may seek to reestablish broken relationships. They need to hear the promises of God's grace in the gospel: "God is greater than our hearts, and he knows everything" (1 John 3:20). They need to hear the promise of eternal life for those who believe in Jesus Christ.

Remembering their Baptism can be of great help to those who are dying. In Baptism the grace of God was promised to them in a very personal way. The New Testament relates Baptism very closely to death:

Do you not know that all of us who have been baptized into Christ Jesus were baptized into his death? We were buried therefore with him by baptism into death, so that as Christ was raised from the dead by the glory of the Father, we too might walk in newness of life. For if we have been united with him in a death like his, we shall certainly be united with him in a resurrection like his (Rom. 6:3-5).

When we physically die, in a sense we are just catching up with our baptism. We share completely in Christ's death in order that we might also participate completely in his life.

Holy Communion, also, is a very significant source of strength to dying persons and their families. A pastor, close relatives, and the patient together can remember the death and resurrection of Christ and receive the gift of his body and blood. Prayers, scripture lessons, hymn texts, and the Lord's Prayer are important reminders that the dying person is not alone, but is among brothers and sisters in the faith and in the loving arms of God himself. A special attempt should be made to read Bible verses or hymns that have been of special significance to the patient.

Physical closeness is very important for those who are taking life's last journey. It is helpful when family members hold a patient's hand to let him or her know they are close by. Some congregations make use of the New Testament tradition of anointing the sick with oil, reminding them that they have been sealed with the cross of Christ through Baptism (James 5:14).

There are many different ways Christians can be of

help to those who are dying. Some actions may seem small and insignificant. Yet God is able to use even the most modest acts of kindness to remind persons of his love in Christ that has conquered death.

Summary

● The New Testament clearly affirms that death is not the end. Those who believe already share in a life that is eternal.

● Our psychological reactions to death and dying are complex. Several stages are usually involved.

● We cannot "practice" dying, but it is important that we develop a sense of familiarity with death. By learning to die, we are learning to live.

● It is extremely important that those who are dying not be left alone on the last part of their life journey.

● It is best when all the persons involved in the care of a dying patient work together to help that individual deal with his or her possible death.

● There are many ways Christians can be of help to those who are dying.

For reflection

Who shall separate us from the love of Christ? Shall tribulation, or distress, or persecution, or famine, or nakedness, or peril, or sword? . . . No, in all these things we are more than conquerors through him who loved us. For I am sure that neither death, nor life, nor angels, nor principalities, nor things present, nor things to come, nor powers, nor height, nor depth, nor anything else in all creation, will be able to separate us from the love of God in Christ Jesus our Lord.

Rom. 8:35, 37-39

Do not seek death. Death will find you. But seek the road which makes death a fulfillment.

Dag Hammarskjöld (1905-1961)
Markings
(Alfred A. Knopf, 1964), p. 159

The more we are making advancements in science, the more we seem to fear and deny the reality of death. . . . We use euphemisms, we make the dead look as if they were asleep, we ship the children off to protect them from the anxiety and turmoil around the house if the patient is fortunate enough to die at home, we don't allow children to visit their dying parents in the hospitals, we have long and controversial discussions about whether patients should be told the truth—a question that rarely arises when the dying person is tended by the family physician who has known him from delivery to death and who knows

DEATH AND DYING 385

the weaknesses and strengths of each member of the
family.

Elisabeth Kübler-Ross
On Death and Dying
(Macmillan, 1969), pp. 7-8

While health crisis in a loved one is always a shock,
if we cannot accept the realities of the health crisis or
adapt as fast as the patient does, we tend to act de-
fensively in an apparent effort to protect our own emotions. This is called the Abandonment Syndrome. Almost all patients express fear that their condition will
make them so unacceptable to those around them that
they will be abandoned. Numerous studies have confirmed their fears. . . . No one can pretend to be able
to meet all of a patient's needs. Only as we recognize
our own limitations and work together can we overcome the Abandonment Syndrome. And only as we
work through those things that threaten us emotionally can we adequately respect our own health.

Glen W. Davidson
Living with Dying
(Augsburg, 1975), pp. 23, 25-26

Death is not to be accepted as much as it is to be
overcome. . . . I am angry that sin and death stalk

man—a righteous anger, I pray, that will not be quiet
when men suffer and die. I am comforted only with
the knowledge that God is angry too. So angry that he
submitted himself to the same suffering and death
and overcame this enemy with his power and gives to
us the fruits of his victory. He has invited us to share
in his death and resurrection.

Kent S. Knutson (1924-1973)
Gospel, Church, Mission
(Augsburg, 1976), p. 51

Lord, be my consolation;
Shield me when I must die;
Remind me of thy Passion
When my last hour draws nigh.
These eyes, new faith receiving,
From thee shall never move;
For he who dies believing
Dies safely in thy love.

Paul Gerhardt (1607-1676)
Lutheran Book of Worship 116

24

Judgment and Hope

What hope can we have in our human future? Prior to World War I, there was a great deal of hope in human progress. But the history of the 20th century has shattered these optimistic dreams. Wars, death camps, hunger, and the nuclear threat have destroyed hopes that human beings will experience a modern age of peace and prosperity. Environmental contamination offers us the prospect of suffocating in our own filth and poison.

In the face of such conditions our longing for the fulfillment of God's kingdom becomes ever greater. What is the shape of our hope in God? How will God resolve human history? What form will God's judgment of the world take? What will life in God's fulfilled kingdom be like?

1. What is the biblical basis for hope?

The Old Testament confesses its faith in a God who acts in human history in a saving way. God creates new situations and relationships and remains faithful to his promises. Israel's understanding of history and expectations for the future were derived from faith in the living God. The book of 1 Samuel praises God by saying,

The Lord kills and brings to life;
he brings down to Sheol and raises up.
The Lord makes poor and makes rich;
he brings low, he also exalts.
(2:6-7; see also Deut. 32:39)

This passage was written within the understanding that these things are fulfilled within history, not in a future life. The same thing holds true for Ezekiel's vision of the valley of dry bones (Ezek. 37:1-14): "And he said to me, 'Son of man, can these bones live?'" (v. 3). Had the prophet answered, "Yes, I think so," he would have anticipated God's promise of a future life. Had he said, "No, I don't believe it," he would not have taken God's power into account. Instead, he answered, "O Lord God, thou knowest." The people of Israel believed God was capable of doing things they were not yet able to understand. They believed God would remain faithful even beyond death and grant new life.

The Old Testament contains many imaginative descriptions of future events, especially in such "apocalyptic" books as Ezekiel and Daniel, books that use dramatic and mysterious images to portray the course of world history. Apocalyptic literature forms the bridge between the Old and New Testaments. In it the Old Testament hope for the coming of God and his saving reign takes on universal dimensions. The message of the apocalyptic literature is that God will be victorious in the conflict with all evil powers and raise the dead. The new age, eternity, will burst upon us. A new heaven and a new earth will come into being. At the end of days, God will send his representative, some great figure—Moses or Elijah or the Son of Man, the Messiah—and appoint him king and judge.

In Jesus the promised age has dawned. God fulfilled his promises when he raised him from the dead. According to Paul, Jesus is "the first fruits of those who have fallen asleep" (1 Cor. 15:20). That which will happen to all has already happened to him. In him all will be transformed, all will "put on" a new imperishable life no longer threatened by death. Everyone who believes in Christ is "a new creation" (2 Cor. 5:17): salvation has come; sin is forgiven; new life has begun; the Spirit is at work. This is a beginning that awaits completion. The Holy Spirit is the "seal" and "guarantee" (Rom. 8:23; 2 Cor. 1:22; 5:5; Eph. 1:13-14) for those who believe, the first installment of that which is still outstanding but will surely come.

Christians are not yet in heaven; the world is still the battlefield on which principalities and powers wage their war against Christ. Sin, suffering, and death have already been conquered by Jesus; but in their flight they continue to engage in rearguard skirmishes. Christians experience the forgiveness of

sin; in faith they are able to endure suffering and
death; in hope they await the world to come.

The early Christians thought Jesus would soon return to complete all things. All attempts to calculate
or determine the exact time of the world's end, however, have failed. Jesus himself said, "Of that day or
that hour no one knows, not even the angels in heav-
en, nor the Son, but only the Father" (Mark 13:32).
All of the descriptions of the end times found in the
New Testament should be read with this in mind
(see Mark 13; Luke 21; Revelation). The New Testament does not provide us with the possibility of putting together a "schedule of coming events" or a
"timetable for eternity." Instead we are admonished
to "take heed," "watch," and "be ready" (Mark 13:
33-37; Matt. 24:42-44; 25:13; Luke 12:35-40; 21:36; 1
Thess. 5:1-10).

2. How will we be judged?

The Bible says, "It is appointed for men to die once,
and after that comes judgment" (Heb. 9:27). The one
who judges us is the one to whom we owe our existence, who has supported us and upheld us throughout our lifetimes. The story about the last judgment in
Matt. 25:31-46 expresses what the New Testament
means by "judgment according to works" (see 2 Cor.
5:10; Rev. 20:12). God can tell whether we belong to
him or not by our actions toward others. Those who
believe in Jesus Christ can be recognized by the

fruits of their faith: "A sound tree cannot bear evil fruit, nor can a bad tree bear good fruit" (Matt. 7:18). Salvation comes through faith, but faith does not exist without being expressed through works (see James 2:14-26). God is gracious and forgiving toward us, yet he still judges us by what we have done. If we belong to Jesus Christ, then Christ will have produced the fruits of faith in us.

3. What is the resurrection of the dead?

The New Testament asserts that the resurrection of the dead has already begun with the resurrection of Jesus. The earliest witness to this truth is found in 1 Corinthians 15, where Paul strongly states the importance of Jesus' resurrection for Christians. Because Christ was raised, we too will be raised.

Resurrection from the dead embraces both continuity and discontinuity at the same time. In other words, earthly life and the new life that God gives us have something to do with each other, yet the new life God gives is something quite different from the life we have known. Paul used the image of sown seeds to describe the resurrection:

What is sown is perishable, what is raised is imperishable. It is sown in dishonor, it is raised in glory. Is is sown in weakness, it is raised in power. It is sown a physical body, it is raised a spiritual body (1 Cor. 15:42-44).

To be a whole person is to have a body. This is also true in the resurrection of the dead. We will be given new bodies, though we shall still be the same persons.

The biblical doctrine of the resurrection of the body is different from immortality of the soul. The New Testament understands resurrected life not as a disembodied existence, but as a new kind of life that includes the physical dimension. There are different interpretations of what happens to our conscious awareness between the time of death and the resurrection. Paul spoke of death as "sleep" and of being "with Christ" (1 Cor. 15:20; Phil. 1:23; 1 Thess. 4:15). Whether believers pass from death to life without being aware of the time in between, or whether they do enjoy conscious communion with Christ, we can take comfort in the promise that all who belong to Christ will be raised, as he was, in a resurrected body. That body will be new and whole, and yet bear some relationship to our present physical existence.

Resurrection will not be just the privilege of individual human beings. God's resurrection of the dead must be seen as part of his renewal of all creation. "The creation itself will be set free from its bondage to decay and obtain the glorious liberty of the children of God" (Rom. 8:21). "I saw a new heaven and a new earth; for the first heaven and the first earth had passed away" (Rev. 21:1). The world is not an accidental arena of human activity that will one day simply disappear; it is to be completed along with the human race. The biblical image of a "new heaven" and a "new earth" points beyond the present existence to a final consummation of all things.

4. What is "eternal life"?

The New Testament describes eternal life on the new earth with numerous images that express joy, fulfillment, and community:

- a bridegroom awaiting his bride
- a marriage feast
- the new Jerusalem
- living water
- the tree of life
- seeing God face to face

For Christians, the final goal is not death, but eternal life. The form it will take is beyond every imagination. It is impossible for us to conceive of anything that exists beyond death, so the Bible speaks of eternal life in images that come from our life. God will "wipe away every tear from their eyes, and death shall be no more, neither shall there be mourning nor crying nor pain any more" (Rev. 21:4).

According to the Bible, eternal life includes life in community with other human beings. The popular imagination has sometimes thought of eternity as a boring, unchanging existence. Eternity, however, is not simply an endless continuation of time; it is more

like fulfilled time—time where the minutes fly by, as
they do for lovers who hardly notice their passing.
Eternal life has already begun for those who believe
in Christ. Life with God is not boring now, and we
can be confident that it will not be so in the future.

The New Testament describes the glory of eternal
life by contrasting it with life's painful experiences:
guilt, suffering, sickness, death, the groaning of creation, war, and poverty. In the new creation, says
Paul, God will be "everything to every one" (1 Cor.
15:28).

Summary

● In Jesus all will be transformed, all will "put on"
a new imperishable life no longer threatened by death.

● Sin, suffering, and death have already been conquered by Jesus; but in their flight they continue to
engage in rearguard skirmishes.

● The New Testament does not provide us with the
possibility of putting together a "schedule of coming
events" or a "timetable for eternity."

● The one who judges us is the one to whom we
owe our existence, who has supported us and upheld
us throughout our lifetimes.

● Resurrection from the dead embraces both continuity and discontinuity at the same time.

● For Christians, the final goal is not death, but
eternal life.

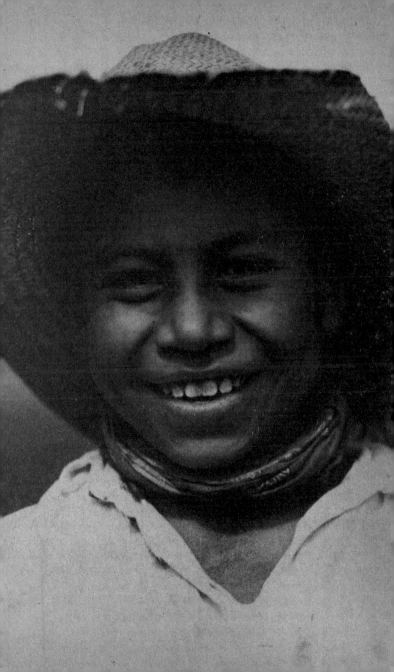

For reflection

Behold, I create new heavens and a new earth;
and the former things shall not be remembered
or come into mind.
But be glad and rejoice for ever
in that which I create;
for behold, I create Jerusalem a rejoicing,
and her people a joy.

Isa. 65:17-18

So all the defencelessness of God's Son and his
grace is a prophecy for his day, for the open Lordship
of God, which here has only begun, and is only se-
cretly present, while he waits at the back door of the
world as a scorned Lazarus, because the rich lord in
the house does not want him to pass his threshold. It
[the open Lordship of God] waits and trembles in
secret power; for all belongs to it. It has trickled already through the framework of the house; and a
tremor as of abysmal powers shakes the pillars and
facades again and again. But the rich man thinks that
it is the stamping of his mighty foot that does this.
And he lays costly carpets on the stone, so that the
growling of the depths no longer disturbs him.

Helmut Thielicke
Between God and Satan
(Eerdmans, 1960), p. 74

Finish then thy new creation,
Pure and spotless let us be;
Let us see thy great salvation
Perfectly restored in thee!
Changed from glory into glory,
Till in heav'n we take our place,
Till we cast our crowns before thee,
Lost in wonder, love, and praise!

Charles Wesley (1707-1788)
Lutheran Book of Worship 315

Men and women are called to enduring hope. True
hope is not based on the ebb and flow of our feelings.
Nor does it come from success in life. True hope—
which means the hope that endures and sustains us—
is based on God's call and command. We are called to
hope. It is a command: a command to resist death. It
is a call: the call to divine life.

Jürgen Moltmann
Experiences of God
(Fortress, 1980), p. 19

Obedience, then, is not the condition of entrance
into the Kingdom of God. Yet, in another sense, condition of entrance it is, in that by it is signified the willingness and the desire to enter. What is more, it is

the seal of him who *has* entered. . . . Christ's own are those who have fed the hungry, clothed the naked, shown mercy to the prisoner and outcast—who have, in short, done the works of Christ (Matt. 25:31-46). Those who have not, whatever their profession and creed, simply are none of his. It does no good to hail him "Lord, Lord," to honor his name in doctrine, hymn, and prayer, if one does not obey him (Matt. 7:21-23).

John Bright
The Kingdom of God
(Abingdon, 1953), pp. 220-221

Come,
Lord,
and cover me with the night.
Spread Your grace over us
as you assured us You would do.
Your promises are more
than all the stars in the sky;
Your mercy is deeper than the night.
Lord,
it will be cold.
The night comes with its breath of death.
Night comes,
the end comes,
but Jesus Christ comes also.
Lord,

we wait for Him
day and night.
Amen.

African prayer, Fritz Pawelzik, ed.
I Sing Your Praise All the Day Long
(© 1967 by Friendship Press), p. 62
Used by permission.